The Incredible
JOURNEY

Published by
The Bible Reading Fellowship
15 The Chambers, Vineyard
Abingdon OX14 3FE
United Kingdom
Tel: +44 (0)1865 319700
Email: enquiries@brf.org.uk
Website: www.brf.org.uk
BRF is a Registered Charity

ISBN 978 0 85746 003 5
First published 2011
10 9 8 7 6 5 4 3 2 1 0
All rights reserved

Acknowledgments
Unless otherwise stated, scripture quotations are taken from the Holy Bible, New International Version, copyright © 1973, 1978, 1984 by International Bible Society, and are used by permission of Hodder & Stoughton Publishers, a member of the Hachette Livre Group UK. All rights reserved. 'NIV' is a registered trademark of International Bible Society. UK trademark number 1448790 • Scripture quotations taken from The Holy Bible, Today's New International Version, copyright © 2004 by International Bible Society. Used by permission of Hodder & Stoughton Publishers, a member of the Hachette Livre Group UK. All rights reserved. 'TNIV' is a registered trademark of International Bible Society • New English Bible copyright © 1961, 1970 by Oxford University Press and Cambridge University Press • Revised English Bible with the Apocrypha copyright © 1989 by Oxford University Press and Cambridge University Press • Scripture quotations from THE MESSAGE. Copyright © by Eugene H. Peterson 1993, 1994, 1995. Used by permission of NavPress Publishing Group • The Living Bible copyright © 1971 by Tyndale House Publishers • Scriptures taken from The Amplified Bible, Old Testament copyright © 1965, 1987 by The Zondervan Corporation • Scripture quotations marked (ESV) are from The Holy Bible, English Standard Version, published by HarperCollins Publishers © 2001 Crossway Bibles, a division of Good News Publishers. Used by permission. All rights reserved.

A catalogue record for this book is available from the British Library

Printed in Singapore by Craft Print International Ltd

The paper used in the production of this publication was supplied by mills that source their raw materials from sustainably managed forests. Soy-based inks were used in its printing and the laminate film is biodegradable.

The Incredible
JOURNEY
Christmas from Genesis to Jesus

Steve Brady

Contents

22–28 December: Arriving on time

29 December–4 January: Journeying on

5–6 January: Homeward bound

Introduction

For as long as I can remember, I have loved cars, coaches and buses—the last, no doubt, influenced by my dad's being a bus driver for nearly 40 years. In addition, my first job on leaving school was with Liverpool City Transport—buses! One consequence is that I have always enjoyed travel, both the journey as well as the destination. I regularly clock up thousands of miles every year by road, usually in connection with being both a minister and the principal of a theological college. Business and pleasure combined, you might say.

The idea of 'journey' is especially appropriate when we turn to the storyline of the Bible. *The Incredible Journey* is a delightful children's book written by British-born Canadian author Sheila Burnford and published in 1961. It was produced as a Disney film under the same title in 1963 and is the heart-warming adventure shared by two dogs and a cat over a 300-mile journey through the Canadian wilderness back to their beloved owners. The Bible could be described as *The Incredible Journey*, too, but it is not primarily an account of humanity's journey back to God, its beloved owner. It is the very reverse: it is God's incredible journey to the human race, which is, amazingly, still loved in spite of all its rejection of him. It culminates in the coming of Jesus Christ, the incarnate God.

Bishop Tom Wright used a different metaphor when he summed up the narrative of scripture:

The early church saw history as a five-act play, with creation, fall and the story of Israel as the first three acts, and the drama reaching its climax in the fourth act, the events concerning Jesus of Nazareth. The early church itself was living in the fifth act, where the actors are charged with the task and responsibility of improvising the final scenes of the play on the basis of all that has gone before.[1]

There is a real danger of my mixing metaphors at this point. However, I would like to suggest that if we combine Tom Wright's idea of a five-act play with the concept of journey, then we discover that the Bible's story could be entitled *The Long and Winding Road* (to quote my fellow Liverpudlian Sir Paul McCartney's famous song). Over the next weeks' readings, we will discover that this particular journey has five waypoints to it, and the road is anything but straightforward. Sometimes it appears to loop back on itself, creating a sense of déjà vu. At other times it is a comparatively straight run.

So, inevitably, there is a starting out, and that will take us all the way back to the dawn of time as we know it, to a beautiful created world and garden where our journey begins in Genesis 1 and 2. All is well here: the skies are blue, the weather good, and the prospects for the adventure ahead are brilliant. All too soon, however, as the narrative turns into Genesis 3, we encounter a radical 'crashing badly'. A major incident has occurred on the motorway at Genesis Junction 3. Roadblocks, diversions and huge signs warning of congestion ahead quickly begin to appear. After such a major 'accident', one phrase summarises the ensuing Old Testament odyssey: detouring often. The diversionary route indicated from the crash scene is not one where even A-class roads are the normal route. The travelogue records some, where heroes and heroines appear, but there are other times when it is not merely country roads but dirt tracks that become the norm, even driving off-road completely. At times, it feels as if a cul-de-sac has been entered, out of which the driver will need to reverse. We will not be able to enter all these nooks and crannies, of course, but there will be a passing comment or more on our whistlestop tour through this part of the terrain.

At one point, the satnav system appears to have closed down completely. No new voice is heard and no fresh instructions are given. The maps that Israel had been divinely provided with, and the moral compass acquired through painful experience as a nation, will need to be rigorously studied and heeded. From Malachi to Matthew is a long journey in the Bible, comprising some 400 'silent years', as they are sometimes called. Home seems like a distant memory and an illusory prospect. Then, quite suddenly and unexpectedly for many on the journey, there is light, heavenly light, coming from a stable and overshadowing a Davidic town, Bethlehem. At last, at least some are cheering. The travellers' map had pointed to this place where the long-awaited deliverer-king would be found. Soon his arriving on time would herald the end to detours, meanderings, being lost and far from home. His coming as a baby king did not please everyone. Nevertheless, here at last, surely, the final end of the journey will be in sight. Well, not quite.

The coming of the king, and the way he intends to deal with the impasse between earth and heaven through his dying and rising again, will form the next part of what turns out to be the journeying on of a hugely expanded group of travellers. No longer will they be predominately of one ethnic group. All nations and all sorts of people are now invited to be pilgrims, to travel from this world to God's everlasting kingdom, empowered by the king's own Spirit all the way. For that part of our adventure, we fast-forward to the wonderful and mysterious book of Revelation, with just one or two detours en route.

So, as we begin our journey through these next weeks, we need to be prepared for some of the 'long and winding road' ahead—but the effort, I believe, will be well worthwhile. After that, we will just have time to make one final stop. In 1993, the film *The Incredible Journey* was remade. It was called *Homeward Bound: The Incredible Journey*. So our final two meditations will take up the theme of homeward bound. For everyone lost and losing it, sinful and stupid, confused and confounded, injured by life and broken by circumstances, disadvantaged by birth, nationality, gender, class or whatever, the Lord Jesus has come to take us home to God. Homeward bound is the culmination of The Greatest Story Ever Told— the journey God himself has taken in entering our world in Jesus Christ to bring us home to his. I pray you will enjoy the ride!

1–7 December

STARTING OUT

Science has no need of purpose… all the extraordinary, wonderful richness of the world can be expressed as growth from the dunghill of purposeless interconnected corruption.

PETER ATKINS, PROFESSOR OF CHEMISTRY, UNIVERSITY OF OXFORD

I am not postulating a 'god of the gaps', a god merely to explain the things that science has not yet explained. I am postulating a God to explain why science explains; I do not deny that science explains, but I postulate God to explain why science explains.

RICHARD SWINBURNE, EMERITUS PROFESSOR OF PHILOSOPHY, UNIVERSITY OF OXFORD

In my view, the question of origin seems to be left unanswered if we explore it from a scientific point of view. Thus, I believe there is a need for some religious or metaphysical explanation. I believe in the concept of God and in his existence.

CHARLES TOWNES, NOBEL PRIZE FOR PHYSICS, 1964[2]

Reports that say that something hasn't happened are always interesting to me, because as we know, there are known knowns; there are things we know we know. We also know there are known unknowns; that is to say we know there are some things we do not know. But there are also unknown unknowns—the ones we don't know we don't know.

DONALD RUMSFELD, SECRETARY OF DEFENCE 2001–06,
UNITED STATES OF AMERICA[3]

1 December

God

In the beginning God created the heavens and the earth.
Now the earth was formless and empty, darkness was over
the surface of the deep, and the Spirit of God was hovering
over the waters. And God said, 'Let there be light,' and there
was light. God saw that the light was good, and he separated
the light from the darkness. God called the light 'day', and
the darkness he called 'night.' And there was evening, and
there was morning—the first day. And God said, 'Let there
be an expanse between the waters to separate water from
water.' So God made the expanse and separated the water
under the expanse from the water above it. And it was so.
God called the expanse 'sky'. And there was evening, and
there was morning—the second day. And God said, 'Let the
water under the sky be gathered to one place, and let dry
ground appear.' And it was so. God called the dry ground
'land,' and the gathered waters he called 'seas.' And God
saw that it was good. Then God said, 'Let the land produce
vegetation: seed-bearing plants and trees on the land that
bear fruit with seed in it, according to their various kinds.'
And it was so. The land produced vegetation: plants bearing
seed according to their kinds and trees bearing fruit with
seed in it according to their kinds. And God saw that it was

good. And there was evening, and there was morning—the third day.
Genesis 1:1–13

'In the beginning God' is the dramatic opening assertion of the Bible: God's relationship to his world and people, time and eternity, heaven and earth, and all there is and ever will be flows out of that phrase. No other starting point, no apologies, no philosophical arguments for God's existence are presented, simply the fact that before the start of anything, God already was. Here is the bold claim that behind everything that there is ('the heavens and the earth' being a catch-all phrase) stands a magnificent, eternal, personal and utterly unique Creator God. A prophet will later record God's own question: 'To whom will you compare me or count me equal? To whom will you liken me that we may be compared?' (Isaiah 46:5). The psalmist's reply is apt: 'There is none like you, O Lord' (Psalm 86:8).

The significance of the word 'created' should not be overlooked. In its context here, it carries the implication of what theologians term *creatio ex nihilo*, creation out of nothing. God did not rearrange pre-existing materials or manipulate eternal matter. Out of generous love and in infinite wisdom, he brought into existence all that there is, visible and invisible. The world depends on God, not the other way round. As Archbishop of Canterbury William Temple used to say, 'God minus the world equals God; the world minus God equals nothing.' [4]

Such claims are not unchallenged, of course. Over the last 150 years in particular, in measure as a response to the publication of Charles Darwin's *On the Origin of Species* in 1859, these early chapters of Genesis have been massively criticised, raising doubts and fears for many believers. 'Descended from the apes! My dear, let us hope that it is not true, but if it is, let us pray that it will not become generally known': such were the sentiments of the wife of the Bishop of Worcester when she heard of Darwin's book.[5] However, 'generally known' this view has become. Today, writers like Richard Dawkins, Christopher Hitchens and a host of others delight to lampoon those believers who think that 'creation' offers any clue to a 'creator'. Such naivety is viewed as being on a par with the belief in a flat earth or fairies at the bottom of the garden.

In reality, it is not a matter of 'faith versus science' or 'faith or science'. These are unnecessary antitheses, since there are many committed Christians who are also able scientists.[6] Whatever else these opening chapters of the Bible intend to teach us (a great deal, as I hope we'll see), if we listen attentively to Genesis we begin to discover 'The Big Message' rather than letting it be drowned out by theories relating to 'The Big Bang'.

What should we hear from Genesis 1? In a fledgling sermon, 'God's relation to the world', written when he was barely in his 20s, Martin Luther King Jr (1929–68) made three telling points: God created the world; God conserves the world; God will transform the world.[7] How do we know God created the world? 'By faith we understand that the universe was formed at God's command, so that what is seen was not made out of what was visible,' says Hebrews 11:2. So the big question is whether the world just 'is', or is dependent on a Creator God. Either way, the answer requires faith in someone or something. That 'God conserves the world' is a reminder that we are not just left on our own: the world around us, though often seemingly haphazard, is still under divine control. Finally, to the question 'Is this world doomed?' the answer that 'God will transform the world' is an antidote to pessimism about the earth's future: it is not irrevocably doomed! To any 'formless and empty' creation or individual, he can say, 'Let there be light' and allow that light to 'shine in our hearts', as Paul puts it (2 Corinthians 4:6), echoing this narrative.

Reflection

If Genesis reminds us of the God who creates and sustains his world, the rest of the Bible's story will tell us how he intends ultimately to transform his world. Thankfully, that includes individuals, created and sustained by God and called in Christ to personal transformation. No one need stay the way they are!

2 December

Starstruck

And God said, 'Let there be lights in the expanse of the sky to separate the day from the night, and let them serve as signs to mark seasons and days and years, and let them be lights in the expanse of the sky to give light on the earth.' And it was so. God made two great lights—the greater light to govern the day and the lesser light to govern the night. He also made the stars. God set them in the expanse of the sky to give light on the earth, to govern the day and the night, and to separate light from darkness. And God saw that it was good. And there was evening, and there was morning—the fourth day. And God said, 'Let the water teem with living creatures, and let birds fly above the earth across the expanse of the sky.' So God created the great creatures of the sea and every living and moving thing with which the water teems, according to their kinds, and every winged bird according to its kind. And God saw that it was good. God blessed them and said, 'Be fruitful and increase in number and fill the water in the seas, and let the birds increase on the earth.' And there was evening, and there was morning—the fifth day.

Genesis 1:14–23

He heals the brokenhearted and binds up their wounds. He determines the number of the stars and calls them each by name.
Psalm 147:3–4

From time immemorial, the stars have fascinated people. Many did and still do believe that they directly affect human beings' activities and destinies because, in some way or other, stars are deities, alongside the sun and moon. Astrology is the name for it. In stark contrast, the Bible can call on the sun, moon and stars to 'praise the name of the Lord, for he commanded and they were created' (Psalm 148:5). So, this opening chapter of Genesis may be viewed as a powerful polemic against any notion that God needed their help: 'God made two great lights—the greater light to govern the day and the lesser light to govern the night', not even giving the sun or moon the courtesy of a name. Then, almost as an afterthought, we read, 'He also made the stars' (v. 16).

It is only in recent times, with the advantage of the Hubble space telescope and the like, that we have begun to appreciate more fully the astonishing claims wrapped up in that statement. Our galaxy, the Milky Way, is composed of one hundred billion stars. That's 100,000,000,000: I'm feeling dizzy already! Some astronomers think there are twice that number. Our nearest 'star neighbour' is Proxima Centauri, 4.3 light years away—a mere thousand billion miles. And how many galaxies are there? At least another one hundred billion. So how many stars in the universe? That's right—a lot! (Ten billion trillion, approximately!) Astronomy is the name for it.

The foregoing is simultaneously mind-boggling and heart-warming. It is mind-boggling because we are reminded that the God of the Bible is no little tin-pot deity: 'He determines the number of the stars, and calls them each by name', proclaims the psalmist. No human individual can count the stars, but God knows the name of every one of them. If my arithmetic is correct, there are enough stars in the universe for every person on earth to own over 1.5 trillion each! But the real heart-warmer is the psalm's preceding verse. The God whose power and greatness are incalculable is not too busy to be bothered with the likes of us, for 'he heals the broken-hearted and binds up their wounds'.

Herein lies both the majesty and the mercy of our God: in the words of the old song, 'he's got the whole world in his hands'— and the universe too. Yet he is not so preoccupied as to ignore a child's prayer, a griefstricken widow's tears or a penitent's cry for mercy. Later in the Bible's unfolding drama, a particular star will guide seekers to a child who is the hope of the world. Were they astrologers or astronomers? Wasn't there a blurring of those lines of demarcation back then? Whatever the case, we can assert that any star, whether in science or science-fiction, that leads away from the Christ-child is always a wandering star, and any star that points to Jesus is always worth following. Wise men and women know that.

Reflection

The stars shine over the mountains;
The stars shine over the sea.
The stars look up to the Mighty God;

And the stars look down on me.
The stars may shine for a million years—
A million years and a day:
But God and I shall live, and love,
When the stars have passed away![8]

3 December

Image bearers

And God said, 'Let the land produce living creatures according to their kinds: livestock, creatures that move along the ground, and wild animals, each according to its kind.' And it was so. God made the wild animals according to their kinds, the livestock according to their kinds, and all the creatures that move along the ground according to their kinds. And God saw that it was good. Then God said, 'Let us make man in our image, in our likeness, and let them rule over the fish of the sea and the birds of the air, over the livestock, over all the earth, and over all the creatures that move along the ground.'

So God created man in his own image, in the image of God he created him; male and female he created them.

God blessed them and said to them, 'Be fruitful and increase in number; fill the earth and subdue it. Rule over the fish of the sea and the birds of the air and over every living creature that moves on the ground.' Then God said, 'I give you every seed-bearing plant on the face of the whole earth and every tree that has fruit with seed in it. They will be yours for food. And to all the beasts of the earth and all the birds of the air and all the creatures that move on the

ground—everything that has the breath of life in it—I give every green plant for food.' And it was so. God saw all that he had made, and it was very good. And there was evening, and there was morning—the sixth day.
Genesis 1:24–31

The immense vastness of the universe, the incredible diversity of life on earth and the dawning reality of our own seeming insignificance sharpens the focus of the psalmist's question: 'What is man?' (Psalm 8:4). The artist Paul Gauguin (1848–1903) captured the human predicament brilliantly in perhaps his greatest masterpiece: Where do we come from? What are we? Where are we going? In the three sweeping, integrated scenes, we see, on the painting's right, a baby and three young women, indicating nearness to the beginning and mystery of life. In the centre, among others, two women converse about life, near to a confused man and a youth plucking fruit. In the last section, a young woman sits next to an old woman who is nearing death. A strange white bird, a symbol of the unknown after death, completes the scenery. Sadly, there's no record that Gauguin found any answers to his questions.

Thankfully, though, Genesis 1 provides answers that put us in our place. Where do we come from? From a Creator's hand, whoever we are. We are made 'in the image and likeness of God... male and female'. Bound into that phrase is a primary idea that there is the possibility of relationship with the God who made us. This gives human beings immense value, dignity, significance and worth. In a real sense, there are no ordinary people. The God who numbers the stars, as we considered yesterday, has no problem knowing everyone on planet earth, and inviting all into a loving relationship with him.

What are we? For some, we are no more than an accidental coincidence on a minor speck of interstellar dust, the product of blind evolutionary forces. For the biblical writers, we are far more. We are, to use a piece of jargon, 'psychophysical entities', with minds that can think, bodies that can move and imaginations that can transcend our circumstances and conceptualise the incon-ceivable—like the 'dark energy' that astrophysicists theorise accounts for 75 per cent of all matter in the universe, though it cannot be seen or touched. We are meant to be here. We are made for this world and vice versa.

Where are we going? This is one of life's ultimate questions, and the story line of the Bible will return to it again and again. One answer quickly thunders from Genesis when humans turn from their Creator: 'Dust you are and to dust you will return' (3:19). Further answers will come in due time, mysteriously prefaced by Enoch's experience as a man who 'walked with God; then he was no more, because God took him away' (Genesis 5:24; Hebrews 11:5). Eventually, one will appear of whom it is said that he is 'the image of the invisible God' (Colossians 1:15). Through his cross and resurrection, Jesus deals with humanity's broken image and can transform us 'into his likeness with ever-increasing glory' (2 Corinthians 3:18).

The Westminster Shorter Catechism has been used in various denominations for over 350 years. Its first question asks, 'What is the chief end of man [and woman]?' The reply is magnificent: 'Man's chief end is to glorify God, and to enjoy him forever'. Where do we come from? A Creator God's hand. What are we? Creatures made in his image and here to glorify him. Where are we going? Through Jesus, we are invited to 'enjoy him forever'.

Reflection

We are 'nothing but fat enough for seven bars of soap, iron enough for one medium-sized nail, sugar enough to fill seven cups of tea, lime enough to whitewash one chicken coop, phosphorus enough to tip 2200 matches, magnesium enough for one dose of salts, potash enough to explode one toy crane, and sulphur enough to rid one dog of fleas.'[9] *How does Genesis 1's account of people help to counter the 'nothing but' reductionism of that statement?*

4 December

Rest

Thus the heavens and the earth were completed in all their vast array. By the seventh day God had finished the work he had been doing; so on the seventh day he rested from all his work. And God blessed the seventh day and made it holy, because on it he rested from all the work of creating that he had done.

Genesis 2:1–3

Remember the Sabbath day by keeping it holy. Six days you shall labour and do all your work, but the seventh day is a Sabbath to the Lord your God. On it you shall not do any work, neither you, nor your son or daughter, nor your manservant or maidservant, nor your animals, nor the alien within your gates. For in six days the Lord made the heavens and the earth, the sea, and all that is in them, but he rested on the seventh day. Therefore the Lord blessed the Sabbath day and made it holy.

Exodus 20:8–11

Before becoming a Christian in my teenage years, I can only say that I had a very relaxed approach to life. It is hard for me to remember getting up much before midday on weekends and school holidays. One of the effects of conversion, for me, was discovering not only mornings but also work. Life now had a purpose as I found I owed my life to one who had given his for me. I quickly found that every day could be full, and life could be lived at a gallop. Days off and holidays? Obviously just for wimps. There was a downside, however—times when I simply hit the buffers, and tiredness and a hard-to-define depression would kick in.

One notable occasion, when I was a theology under-graduate, brought some sanity to my frenetic lifestyle. I had just finished a week of intensive mission in the south of England and drove home overnight to my native Liverpool to commence my next evangelistic week of mission, starting that Sunday. Monday came and my head was swimming. I felt 'blue' and wondered how I was to get through the week. At the end of that evening's meeting, a smallish man with a clipped English accent approached me. 'Young man, are you obeying the fourth commandment?' he asked. I was so tired, I did not know how many commandments there were, never mind what was number four! Colonel Bell went on to inform me that when he served in India, in the time of Mahatma Gandhi, the latter took every Monday off. 'Don't you think, if Gandhi, with [at that time] six hundred million people to look after, could take a day off, you could? Hmm?'

God's resting on the seventh day from all his work is a stark reminder that the God who 'will not grow tired or weary' (Isaiah 40:28) nevertheless has stitched into the fabric of creation both work and rest, ebb and flow, or, in a word, rhythm. This sabbath principle was deeply ingrained into Israel's law, based both on creation (as in our reading from Exodus above) and redemption.[10] One day per week in ancient Israel, everyone was visibly reminded that God was both creator and redeemer, as daily chores and other responsibilities were laid aside. One of the reasons recorded later for Israel's 70-year exile was that its land might enjoy 'its Sabbath rests' (2 Chronicles 36:21).

Is this, then, a clarion call to traditional sabbath observance? Is Sunday to be 'glum day', as some of us experienced in our childhoods, when it was a 'sin' to play with a toy? Or is it to be what it has become for many of our neighbours—another 'fun day' with no time or thought for God? 'The Sabbath was made for man, not man for the Sabbath', according to Jesus (Mark 2:27), so there is an abiding principle that many of us need desperately to discover. We do not need merely 'time off' or 'time out' but time with God. Every sabbath, Israel was reminded that there was a priority beyond making a living. It was finding a life in God. Every day may be a 'sabbath' when we respond to Christ's invitation: 'Come to me, all you who are weary and burdened, and I will give you rest' (Matthew 11:28). For, as Hebrews 4:1–11 reminds us, such 'sabbath rest' is ultimately salvation itself, procured by and found in Jesus. Now that's a rest well worth taking.

Reflection

On one occasion, Jesus said to his disciples, 'Come ye yourselves apart into a desert place, and rest a while' (Mark 6:31, KJV). As someone wisely put it, 'If you don't take time to 'come apart' with Jesus, you may simply come apart!'

5 December

Stewardship

Then God said, 'Let us make man in our image, in our likeness, and let them rule over the fish of the sea and the birds of the air, over the livestock, over all the earth, and over all the creatures that move along the ground.' … God blessed them and said to them, 'Be fruitful and increase in number; fill the earth and subdue it. Rule over the fish of the sea and the birds of the air and over every living creature that moves on the ground.'

Genesis 1:26, 28

The Lord God formed the man from the dust of the ground and breathed into his nostrils the breath of life, and the man became a living being. Now the Lord God had planted a garden in the east, in Eden; and there he put the man he had formed. And the Lord God made all kinds of trees grow out of the ground—trees that were pleasing to the eye and good for food. In the middle of the garden were the tree of life and the tree of the knowledge of good and evil… The Lord God took the man and put him in the Garden of Eden to work it and take care of it.

Genesis 2:7–9, 15

The earth is the Lord's, and everything in it, the world, and all who live in it.
Psalm 24:1

It was nearly 40 years ago, but I clearly remember a young medical student telling me that one of her professors had warned his students about the dangers of 'CFCs' (chlorofluorocarbons). This chemical, then used in deodorants, hairsprays and other aerosols as well as elsewhere, was both contaminating the atmosphere and opening holes in the ozone layer. Back then, to many of us, such warnings appeared to be alarmist at best and nonsense at worst. How times have changed!

Some verses in today's first reading have often been cited as a *carte blanche* for poisoning the seas, polluting the air, exploiting the animal kingdom and ravaging the earth. The result is that there is now a growing army of people concerned about our physical habitat. At one extreme, there are the 'eco-warriors', determined to save the planet, whatever it takes. Somewhere in the middle, many of us are increasingly aware of the devastation we are causing to our environment and our need to do our bit by wisely recycling all we can, being aware of our 'carbon footprints' and acting responsibly. At the other extreme, there are scientists like Sir James Lovelock, who think that we are almost beyond the point of redemption. Writing in *The Independent*, he argued that 'billions of us will die and the few breeding pairs of people that survive will be in the Arctic where the climate remains tolerable'—all by the end of this century.[11]

Depleted ozone layers, melting polar ice caps, raised sea

levels, a growing world population with, seemingly, fewer and fewer resources to go round—do global disaster and human extinction await us? These are questions to which we will return later. What the narrative in Genesis does not assert, however, is that 'rule' or 'dominion' (KJV) should be used as synonyms for 'reckless disregard', 'domination', 'exploitation', 'devastation' or 'destruction' of the inhabited world. The picture in Genesis 2 that complements and fills out the story of our creation in Genesis 1 is, in itself, a protest against such reductionism. Adam is placed in a beautiful garden and is presented as 'the park keeper at work',[12] taking care of what God had created, not destroying it. Sadly, another story of human rebellion will occur in Genesis 3, but the Bible never allows us to forget that 'The earth is the Lord's, and everything in it, the world, and all who live in it', as the psalmist boldly asserts (Psalm 24:1). In other words, we are the tenants here, but the 'garden' and the whole 'house' of the world belong to God, their owner, architect and builder.

Recently, my son and daughter-in-law entered into a tenancy agreement. There were pages of fine print, including an inventory of the house, its state of repair and its contents, plus the mutual obligations of both landlord and tenant. Here in Genesis is a creation tenancy agreement. Six times the narrative has reminded us that God's world was 'good' and, finally, that it was 'very good'.[13] If God handed Adam the keys to such a 'very good' world, it is not God's fault that the world is as we now find it. As Genesis asserts and all history will subsequently illustrate, such a state of affairs has a great deal to do with the tenants. Little wonder that we soon read, 'The Lord was grieved that he had made man on the earth, and his heart was filled with pain' (Genesis 6:6). One day, that heartache became incarnate in 'a man of sorrows, and acquainted with grief' (Isaiah 53:3, ESV), who, with a heart full of pain, wept over a city and died to be the Saviour of the world.[14]

Reflect

Lord, help me to be a good steward and use wisely whatever time, talents and treasure you have entrusted to me. So may your kingdom come and your will be done through me to benefit others in your world, for Jesus' sake, Amen.

6 December

Harmony

Now the Lord God had planted a garden in the east, in Eden; and there he put the man he had formed. And the Lord God made all kinds of trees grow out of the ground—trees that were pleasing to the eye and good for food. In the middle of the garden were the tree of life and the tree of the knowledge of good and evil. A river watering the garden flowed from Eden; from there it was separated into four headwaters. The name of the first is the Pishon; it winds through the entire land of Havilah, where there is gold. (The gold of that land is good; aromatic resin and onyx are also there.) The name of the second river is the Gihon; it winds through the entire land of Cush. The name of the third river is the Tigris; it runs along the east side of Asshur. And the fourth river is the Euphrates. The Lord God took the man and put him in the Garden of Eden to work it and take care of it. And the Lord God commanded the man, 'You are free to eat from any tree in the garden; but you must not eat from the tree of the knowledge of good and evil, for when you eat of it you will surely die.' The Lord God said, 'It is not good for the man to be alone. I will make a helper suitable for him.' Now the Lord God had formed out of the ground all the beasts of the field and all the birds of the air. He brought them to the man to see what he would name them; and whatever the man called each living creature, that was its name. So the man gave names to all the livestock, the birds of the air and all the beasts of the field. But for Adam no suitable helper was found.

Genesis 2:8–20

The kiss of the sun for pardon,
The song of the birds for mirth;
One is nearer God's heart in a garden
Than anywhere else on earth.

This well-known verse from the poem 'God's garden'[15] is found on signs, plaques and ornaments in many gardens in the UK and beyond. As one who loves gardens but hates the task of gardening, I have always been rather perplexed by the verse, not only at a physical but also at a theological level. Allow me to elaborate. The poem's opening couplet mirrors the scene recorded here in Genesis 2:

The Lord God planted a garden
In the first white days of the world.

The picture painted of rivers, trees, animals and birds all living in peace and harmony with humankind is breath-takingly wonderful. It is a scene that finds an echo in the human heart—a form of universal homesickness for a paradise lost. In a world full of pollution, injustice, poverty, crime and war, here is a reminder of what life could be and should be like. At their best, peace movements campaign for such a world, eco-warriors battle for it, animal rights protesters clamour for it and prisoners of conscience yearn for the day when 'righteousness and peace kiss each other' (Psalm 85:10). John Lennon's song 'Imagine' caught the mood of a generation: 'Imagine all the people living life in peace.' It is that wistful longing, seeking for a utopia we feel we have lost. But how have we lost it? Notably, it is not man at the centre of the garden, but 'the tree of life and the tree of the knowledge of good and evil' (Genesis 2:9). It is with reference to the latter that the only prohibition is found: 'You must not eat' from it (v. 17). In other words, humanity's freedom has limits: it must not play God. Genesis records our attempt to do so and its disastrous consequences.

As the Bible's story unfolds, another Adam finally appears: 'the last Adam', according to Paul (1 Corinthians 15:45). Mark's Gospel's opening verses present Jesus not in a garden but a wilderness with wild animals.[16] Here is a telling metaphor of the world we now inhabit—spiritually, a wilderness without God, with untamed forces around and 'Nature, red in tooth and claw'.[17] Later, Matthew records Jesus' battle in the garden of Gethsemane, and Dr Luke adds that 'his sweat was like drops of blood falling to the ground'. John's account of the resurrection finds Christ not only in a garden but being mistaken by Mary Magdalene for the gardener.[18] In the Bible's final chapters, Revelation 21 and 22, we are introduced to a garden city: 'Paradise regained' as John Milton phrased it. One day, 'All shall be well and all shall be well and all manner of thing shall be well,' asserted the medieval mystic Julian of Norwich. Christ, 'The Proper Man' according to Martin Luther, has come to make improper people new again.

So, wherein lies my perplexity with Dorothy Frances Gurney's verse, quoted at the beginning? Well, according to Genesis 1:26–27, it is people who bear God's image. All created life is to be viewed with due respect. But, with due respect, we are actually nearer to God when we are close to our fellow human beings—squashed in a tube train, queuing at a checkout, frustratingly delayed in traffic. However messed up, dysfunctional and exasperating people may be (some much more than others), people really do matter to God. That's why, in Christ, God became one of us, invading our cities of destruction to lead us to his eternal paradise, the garden city of God.

By the way, anyone for gardening?

Reflection

Harmony in God's world may seem like a pipedream at present. At a personal level, it may seem a million miles away from our hearts and homes. Why not take some time to meditate and act on the following promise?

'Do not be anxious about anything, but in everything, by prayer and petition, with thanksgiving, present your requests to God. And the peace of God, which transcends all understanding, will guard your hearts and your minds in Christ Jesus' (Philippians 4:6–7).

7 December

Unity

The Lord God said, 'It is not good for the man to be alone. I will make a helper suitable for him.' Now the Lord God had formed out of the ground all the beasts of the field and all the birds of the air. He brought them to the man to see what he would name them; and whatever the man called each living creature, that was its name. So the man gave names to all the livestock, the birds of the air and all the beasts of the field. But for Adam no suitable helper was found. So the Lord God caused the man to fall into a deep sleep; and while he was sleeping, he took one of the man's ribs and closed up the place with flesh. Then the Lord God made a woman from the rib he had taken out of the man, and he brought her to the man. The man said, 'This is now bone of my bones and flesh of my flesh; she shall be called "woman", for she was taken out of man.'

For this reason a man will leave his father and mother and be united to his wife, and they will become one flesh. The man and his wife were both naked, and they felt no shame.
Genesis 2:18–25

Let's be frank: marriage as an institution in the UK is in some crisis. An article in *The Independent* sought to put things into some perspective: 'Till death do us part: why marriage remains popular',[19] but crises there remain. The summary by one of my friends is worth repetition: 'The average marriage lasts twelve years: four years wedlock, four years deadlock, four years unlock.' Pithy, memorable, humorous and sad. Yet here in Genesis, at the dawn of our time, we are given what theologians like to call a 'creation ordinance'. Like much else described in these opening chapters—work and rest, privilege and stewardship—marriage is both a gift and a responsibility.

We immediately note that marriage is not a mere human convenience or contrivance but God's idea: 'It is not good for man to be alone.' The seeming excursus around the animal and bird kingdoms plays an important role in 'marriage preparation'. There, poignantly, for Adam 'no suitable helper was found'. When preparing couples for marriage, I have often asked them to reflect on whether they really do need to marry. Why? Because some men are already 'happily married' to their career or their sport or whatever, while some women are so committed to their home or their family that the 'game of marriage' is doomed before kick-off time. In contrast, marriage entails a 'leaving', a 'uniting' and a 'becoming one flesh', a kind of three-legged stool for which each leg is important. The three 'legs' entail different but integrated ideas: a public act, so everyone knows the couple is committed to each other and whereby a new family unit is established; an ongoing volitional act to stay together permanently as part of a covenant promise to be faithful to each other 'in sickness and in health' and so on; and a mutual union on many levels of their life together, including sexual relationships. When marriages get into difficulty, it is usually one or more of these 'legs' that has lacked attention.

It is instructive to ask what immediately precedes the phrase, 'The man and his wife were both naked' (v. 25). The usual answer is 'flesh', but actually it is a full stop, a period. Marriage is complete with or without children. That said, Psalm 127:5 reminds us that we are blessed if our 'quiver is full' of children. But a 'government health warning' may be in order here: children may be a 'quiver full', but they are usually also a 'hand full'!

Some people reading the foregoing comments may feel a little excluded, because they are single, divorced, widowed or whatever, and may wish it were otherwise. I recall asking a delightful old lady why she had never married, especially since I could see from yesteryear's photos how beautiful she had been. 'No one ever asked me, Pastor' was her reply, spoken without self-pity but with a tinge of regret. I do not know why some people find a marriage partner easily (sometimes repeatedly so), while others find that the 'gift of singleness'[20] is a gift they did not want. But it would be irresponsible to leave these verses without probing them more deeply. When the apostle Paul wrote about marriage, he specifically quoted from this passage and immediately added, 'This is a profound mystery—but I am talking about Christ and the church' (Ephesians 5:32). Have you ever looked through the wrong end of a telescope? It gives a very different picture than the 'right' end. Our temptation is to assume that the love that a husband and wife should have for each other, looking through the 'right' end, is somehow seen a little more clearly in Christ's love for his people, the

Church. So human love is the original pattern and Christ's love for his people is the copy. In fact, though, it was always the other way round.

Augustine was once asked what God was doing before he created the world. His reply was to the effect that God was preparing a place of punishment for people who asked fatuous questions! It is a legitimate question, though. What was he doing? Among other things, he was preparing to bring people of all sorts and shapes and colours and sizes into his kingdom and love them for ever. They are described in Revelation as 'a great multitude' (7:9), 'prepared as a bride beautifully dressed for her husband' (21:2). Here is a proposal of marriage to Jesus Christ that is not only 'till death us do part'. It is an invitation to an eternal relationship with the God who made us and redeemed us in Christ. All are invited to this wedding; everyone is urgently encouraged to respond personally to such an amazing proposition.

Reflection

Take some time to pray for relationships that you know are under strain at present. Be specific. Are there ways you can help to heal a hurting heart? Sending a text, writing a letter, going out for a coffee, or just being a listening ear? If it is your own heart that is broken, remember, 'The Lord is close to the brokenhearted and saves those who are crushed in spirit' (Psalm 34:18).

NOTES

1   N.T. Wright, 'Jerusalem in the New Testament', in P.W.L. Walker (ed.), *Jerusalem Past and Present in the Purposes of God* (Deo Gloria Trust, 1992), p. 72.
2   Quoted by John C. Lennox, *God's Undertaker: Has Science Buried God?* (Lion Hudson, 2009), pp. 43, 47, 69.
3   Donald Rumsfeld's Briefing for the United States Department of Defence, 12 February 2002.
4   See William Temple, *Nature, Man and God* (Macmillan, 1934), p. 435.
5   From the foreword to Charles Darwin's *On the Origin of Species* (Avenel Books, 1976), p. v.
6   See, for instance, a list of contemporary scientists who are Christians in Lennox, *God's Undertaker*, pp. 22–23. The literature on the wider debate is large and wide-ranging, reflecting different Christian approaches. See, for instance, Denis Alexander, *Creation or Evolution: Do We Have to Choose?* (Monarch, 2008); R.J. Berry and T.A. Noble (eds.), *Darwin, Creation and the Fall* (Apollos, 2009); Francis S. Collins, *The Language of God* (Free Press, 2006); Norman C. Nevin (ed.), *Should Christians Embrace Evolution?* (IVP, 2009).
7   From The Martin Luther King Papers Project, held at Stanford University: mlk-kpp01.stanford.edu/.../Vol6/1948–1954God'sRelationtotheWorld.pdf.
8   Attributed to Robert Louis Stevenson (1850–94).
9   David Watson, *In Search of God* (Falcon, 1974), p. 40.
10 Deuteronomy 5:12–15.
11 James Lovelock, 'The Earth is about to catch a morbid fever that may last as long as 100,000 years', *The Independent* (16 January 2006).
12 David Atkinson, *The Message of Genesis 1—11* (IVP, 1990), p. 60.
13 See Genesis 1:4, 10, 12, 18, 21, 25, 31.
14 See Luke 19:41–44.
15 By Dorothy Frances Gurney (1858–1932).
16 See Mark 1:13.
17 From Alfred, Lord Tennyson's group of cantos entitled *In Memoriam A.H.H.* (1850). This quotation comes from Canto LVI.
18 Matthew 26:36–46; Luke 22:44; John 20:15.
19 Paul Vallely, *The Independent* (16 September 2008).
20 See Matthew 19:10–12 and Paul's discussion in 1 Corinthians 7.

8–14 December

CRASHING BADLY

The condition in which we find ourselves today is not simply one of unhappiness, not merely one in which there is sickness, in which people cheat one another, and so on. It is far more serious than that. According to the Bible we are in a fallen state… The only thing that can be done must be done by God himself, and God has done it.

E.J. YOUNG [1]

C.S. Lewis poignantly expressed the sense of paradise lost that we wistfully experience, when mulling over our memories, as 'only the scent of a flower we have not found, the echo of a tune we have not heard, news from a country we have never yet visited'. [2]

8 December

Temptation

Now the serpent was more crafty than any of the wild animals the Lord God had made. He said to the woman, 'Did God really say, "You must not eat from any tree in the garden"?' The woman said to the serpent, 'We may eat fruit from the trees in the garden, but God did say, "You must not eat fruit from the tree that is in the middle of the garden, and you must not touch it, or you will die."' 'You will not surely die,' the serpent said to the woman. 'For God knows that when you eat of it your eyes will be opened, and you will be like God, knowing good and evil.'
Genesis 3:1–5

An astrophysicist was conducting a lecture tour around the UK. His chauffeur, after hearing the same verbatim lecture for the umpteenth time, remarked that he thought he could now deliver it himself. The professor took up the challenge, they swapped places and the chauffeur duly delivered the lecture almost word-perfectly. Unfortunately for him, he finished five minutes early. The chairperson immediately invited questions. The first question was so complex and convoluted that it brought a gasp of astonishment from the erudite audience. The chauffeur-cum-professor, however, remained composed:

'See that man down there. He's my chauffeur. To illustrate how easy it actually is to answer that question, I'm going to ask him to come up here and do it for me!'

Unlike this 'professor', however, we don't have a chauffeur to answer all the imponderable questions that this chapter of the Bible inevitably raises. Nevertheless, as indicated in the Introduction, as we turn into Genesis 3 we are moving from Act One to Act Two of the Bible's five-act drama, from 'Starting out' to 'Crashing badly' in this incredible travelogue of faith. 'The Fall' is what theologians term the events recorded in Genesis 3. It will be easy to miss the wood for the trees or, more appropriately, the serpent for the foliage. What we can note, however, is that the whole narrative turns on a question, the first in the Bible: 'Did God really say...?'

The purpose of the question, we immediately realise, is not to elicit information but to inject doubt. There is no mention of the serpent's origin here, but its role is clear: it represents both threat and danger to this primeval pair in a created order and garden that were still 'very good' (1:31). Its 'craftiness' lies in a misquotation, which we are to presume is quite deliberate. The permission granted by God to eat to the full from 'any tree in the garden' (2:16) is subtly questioned and changed into 'You must not eat from any tree' (3:1). The woman's initial reply leads to a full-frontal attack—a denial by the serpent of the words of God. 'You will not surely die' is its riposte, whereas God had plainly said, 'You will surely die' (2:17).

How did the serpent become so 'crafty' and seek to oppose God, when all he had made was so good? Where did evil come from? What is its origin? These are questions to which we have no direct answers here, although later the Bible will describe the devil as 'that ancient serpent' (Revelation 12:9; 20:2), echoing this passage. Moreover, the apostle Paul's reference to Satan's conceit suggests to some commentators an echo of the pride of a being who, according to Ezekiel, was 'in Eden, the garden of God'.[3] Does Genesis 3 hint at such supernatural evil? Would the writer be surprised if his readers made such a deduction? Hardly. In a chapter that ends with angelic beings, 'cherubim', guarding the way to the tree of life, supernatural evil would not be at all unexpected. Nevertheless, neither here nor elsewhere does the Bible teach any form of cosmic dualism, such as may be found in certain understandings of Zoroastrianism, where good and evil appear to be both equal and eternal, endlessly battle things out.

At another level, however, we are reading our own story when faced with trial and temptation. The serpent's insinuation is that God is not playing fair with us, that he is a cosmic killjoy who is trying to spoil our fun and limit our freedom. Is he perhaps like the caricature of the old Puritans: 'a Puritan is someone who is deathly afraid that someone, somewhere, is having fun'? So, in spite of all the evidence to the contrary, displayed in God's goodness all around in paradise, the woman chooses to ignore what God has said and prefers to listen to a talking snake, whose credentials she does not check out and whose qualifications are suspect. Eve made her choice when, all the time, she had her husband alongside—who, like the 'chauffeur', could have answered the tempter's question because he had directly heard God's command as recorded in the previous chapter (2:16–17).

Both of them were to live in obedience to God's revealed will, in line with the word God had given them, for therein lay the path to life and liberty.

Here is the ongoing challenge. To whom am I listening? Whose word do I trust? Who's pulling my strings? Contrary to the way Eve was made to feel by the serpent, the Lord's 'commands are not burdensome' (1 John 5:3). In listening to and trusting what our Creator tells us, even when it does not always make immediate sense (why is this one tree's fruit forbidden?), we find the path to life. Do we still feel in need of a chauffeur, someone to answer all our questions and be there at our side? In Jesus Christ, the Christian has an 'advocate' (1 John 2:1, ESV), someone called alongside us to bring us help. Often, we will need to be patient for answers: 'You do not realise now what I am doing, but later you will understand' (John 13:7).[4] But, unlike the serpent's, Jesus Christ's credentials are impeccable: 'This is my Son... Listen to him!' (Matthew 17:5). Do we?

Reflection

Today, like every day, there will be many voices competing for our attention. During a very fraught period in his life, Elijah discovered that God's voice was not in the wind, earthquake or fire, but in 'a gentle whisper' (1 Kings 19:11–12). Ask the Lord to help you listen carefully for his voice of calm today.

9 December

Disobedience

When the woman saw that the fruit of the tree was good for food and pleasing to the eye, and also desirable for gaining wisdom, she took some and ate it. She also gave some to her husband, who was with her, and he ate it. Then the eyes of both of them were opened, and they realised that they were naked; so they sewed fig leaves together and made coverings for themselves. Then the man and his wife heard the sound of the Lord God as he was walking in the garden in the cool of the day, and they hid from the Lord God among the trees of the garden. But the Lord God called to the man, 'Where are you?'

Genesis 3:6–9

'We're having a little quiz,' said the police officer to my friend. 'Can you tell me what that traffic sign means?' 'No entry, Officer,' came the quick and confident reply, followed up by an even faster addition: 'Oh no, I went in that way, didn't I?' 'You've just got the second quiz question right, Sir,' the officer continued.

Which part of the 'No entry' sign did my friend not understand? It was ignored, for whatever reason, and, since ignorance of the law is no excuse, in his case it reaped a good telling off. Here in the garden of Eden, the Lord had only placed one restriction: 'You must not eat from the tree of the knowledge of good and evil' (2:17). The phrase means something like 'the knowledge about everything': in other words, God's way of knowing—omniscience, understanding the infinite, and so. The prohibition reminds us that there are necessary limits to human knowledge. We should not listen to the tempter's suggestion later in the narrative that we will 'be like God, knowing good and evil' (3:5). As the Swiss theologian Karl Barth expressed it many years ago, 'You don't say "God" by saying "Man" with a loud voice!' So, which part of God's 'No entry' sign did Eve not understand?

When it comes to the question 'Why is there evil?' at least some of the answer is hinted at in our text. The serpent introduced the temptation to doubt God, but that did not exonerate the human couple. They still had choices to make. They could exercise their God-given free will. As someone put it, temptation is like the devil knocking at your door; sin is opening the door and letting him in.

That said, it is sheer folly to underestimate the power of temptation. This particular temptation appealed to Eve's physical appetite ('good for food') her aesthetic taste ('pleasing to the eye') and her intellectual pride ('desirable for gaining wisdom'). There's an echo of that trinity of temptation in John's first epistle, where he speaks of 'the lust of the flesh and the lust of the eyes and the pride of life' (1 John 2:16), summarised as worldliness—that is, a life and lifestyle that are under any control except God's.

A wise man once remarked that we never know how bad we are until we try to be good, but the narrative provides no excuses for the guilty pair's behaviour. The verbs plot Eve's rapid downward spiral into disobedience: she 'saw... took... ate'. Moreover, disobedience is always more pleasurable when we can implicate others. So she 'also gave some to her husband... and he ate'. Did he perhaps not know where the ill-gotten fruit had come from? Hardly! He 'was with her', and later in the passage God rebukes him for listening to her and thus being totally complicit in her actions (3:17).

One of the most popular songs of modern times is Paul Anka's 'My way', increasingly played at British funerals in preference to traditional hymns such as 'The Lord's my shepherd'. The lyrics centre round a man facing death and reflecting on his life. He plotted his own course; he did his own thing, sometimes biting off more than he could chew, but he has few regrets. Why? Because the record of his life shows, 'I did it my way!' At one level, there's something endearing and challenging in those sentiments: we were never created to be carbon copies of someone else or merely conformists for conformity's sake. At another level, though, the song's lyrics are utterly tragic. They could appropriately be played over Adam and Eve. They did it their way but the results were catastrophic.

Someone has remarked that the essence of heaven is a world where we say to God, 'Your will be done'; the essence of hell is where God says to us, 'Your will be done!' Already the narrative is beginning to hint at our need of a way out, since we are all naturally wilful. To fast-forward the story, a man once prayed, 'Not as I will, but as you will' (Matthew 26:39). That will of God took Jesus to the cross in order to forgive the likes of this guilty pair in paradise, and a world sunk in its disobedience. Because of that, like the well-known prodigal son, we might use our free will again: 'I *will* set out and go back to my father and say to him: "Father, I have sinned against heaven and against you"' (Luke 15:18). Every returning prodigal son or daughter can then expect a warm embrace and welcome home from the God who, in Jesus, runs to meet us.

Reflection

'Do not let me strive to understand the infinite, but spend my strength in love… My Lord, I leave the infinite to You and ask You to put far from me a love for the tree of knowledge that would keep me from the tree of life.'

CHARLES SPURGEON (1834–92)[5]

10 December

Discovery

Then the man and his wife heard the sound of the Lord God as he was walking in the garden in the cool of the day, and they hid from the Lord God among the trees of the garden. But the Lord God called to the man, 'Where are you?' He answered, 'I heard you in the garden, and I was afraid because I was naked; so I hid.' And he said, 'Who told you that you were naked? Have you eaten from the tree from which I commanded you not to eat?' The man said, 'The woman you put here with me—she gave me some fruit from the tree, and I ate it.' Then the Lord God said to the woman, 'What is this you have done?' The woman said, 'The serpent deceived me, and I ate.'
Genesis 3:8–13

Nothing in all creation is hidden from God's sight. Everything is uncovered and laid bare before the eyes of him to whom we must give account.
Hebrews 4:13

A woman had been pouring out her heart to a wise and kind Christian counsellor. As their time drew to a close, appropriately the counsellor suggested that they now pray together, bringing the woman's heavy load to God and leaving it with him. 'Oh no!' she immediately protested, 'I don't want him to know!'

We smile at her naivety if we know anything of the true and living God: 'Where can I go from your Spirit? Where can I flee from your presence? If I go up to the heavens, you are there; if I make my bed in the depths, you are there,' the psalmist graphically reminds us (Psalm 139:7–8). God's omniscience, his all-knowingness, is both an amazing comfort and a deeply disturbing reality. Almost comically, as the guilty pair hear God's approach, 'they hid from the Lord God among the trees of the garden'. But there is something deeply ironic here, too. As one writer puts it, 'The trees which were meant as the context for their freedom ('You may freely eat of every tree', Genesis 2:16) are now the context of a cover-up. The park becomes a prison. They are trapped in their shame and their guilt.'[6] Yet how foolish to hide from God! There cannot ultimately be a secret sin, since 'everything is uncovered and laid bare before the eyes of him to whom we must give an account'.

Today, however, many people do not believe in such a God. If there is a God, then he must be nice, cosy, easy to domesticate and one who only sees the good in everybody. We might occasionally need him, just as we need an airbag in a car—in cases of emergency only, and, we hope, not too often. As the world-renowned fashion guru Giorgio Armani recently expressed it in an interview, 'I believe there is a God. Sometimes I rely upon him.'[7] Otherwise, we get through life as best we can. But the Christian's God is anything but convenient. His name, 'the Lord', 'Yahweh', means 'I AM

WHO I AM' (Exodus 3:14). That means he is always true to himself. Indeed, he is 'The Lord, the compassionate and gracious God, slow to anger, abounding in love and faithfulness' and yet 'he does not leave the guilty unpunished' because he is 'holy, holy, holy' (Exodus 34:6–7; Isaiah 6:3). So God's questions, 'Where are you? ... Who told you? ... What is this you have done?' are both searching and merciful invitations to come clean with him by a full and frank confession of disobedience. Instead, as the narrative unfolds, and as the saying goes, 'Adam blamed Eve, Eve blamed the serpent, and the serpent did not have a leg to stand on!' Are you hiding something from God? Yourself, perhaps?

The Dufflepuds are comic characters created by C.S. Lewis for *The Voyage of the Dawn Treader*, part of his Chronicles of Narnia. They are slow, dim-witted and more than willing to behave foolishly, constantly fawning over their leader, the Chief Duffer. However, they are supposed to be the servants of the magician Coriakin, whom they mistakenly believe to be a tyrant. In fact, he loves them, seeks to educate them and enables them to survive. Foolishly, they cast one of Coriakin's spells to turn themselves invisible in the mistaken belief that now they are out of sight, they are undetectable. The truth, however, is they make a tremendous thumping noise every time they move around, so Coriakin always knows where they are. Here in the garden of Eden, our forebears act as 'real duffers', losing their access to the tree of life and the joy of a personal relationship with the God who made them and loved them. Thankfully, Jesus said that his mission in coming to earth was 'to seek and save what was lost' (Luke 19:10). Who'd stay a Dufflepud when there is forgiveness with God? Surely that could qualify anyone for the title 'Chief Duffer'.

Reflection

'Search me, O God, and know my heart; test me and know my anxious thoughts. See if there is any offensive way in me, and lead me in the way everlasting' (Psalm 139:23–24).

11 December

Cover up

Then the eyes of both of them were opened, and they realised that they were naked; so they sewed fig leaves together and made coverings for themselves. Then the man and his wife heard the sound of the Lord God as he was walking in the garden in the cool of the day, and they hid from the Lord God among the trees of the garden. But the Lord God called to the man, 'Where are you?' He answered, 'I heard you in the garden, and I was afraid because I was naked; so I hid.' And he said, 'Who told you that you were naked? Have you eaten from the tree that I commanded you not to eat from?'
Genesis 3:7–11

The Lord God made garments of skin for Adam and his wife and clothed them. And the Lord God said, 'The man has now become like one of us, knowing good and evil. He must not be allowed to reach out his hand and take also from the tree of life and eat, and live for ever.' So the Lord God banished him from the Garden of Eden to work the ground from which he had been taken. After he drove the man out, he placed on the east side of the Garden of Eden cherubim and a flaming sword flashing back and forth to guard the way to the tree of life.
Genesis 3:21–24

For many people, 17 June 1972 became a watershed in the history of America. On that day, five men broke into the Democratic National Committee's HQ at the Watergate complex. Their subsequent arrest and further investigations by the Senate Watergate Committee clearly implicated the President himself, Richard Nixon. Notwithstanding his best efforts to cover up the sordid affair, he faced possible trial and conviction. Accordingly, on 9 August 1974, Richard Nixon resigned the office of President of the United States of America. Ever since, 'Watergate' has become a synonym for every attempt to conceal facts and to stonewall in the face of overwhelming evidence of misdemeanour. Why do human beings do such things? Why are we so quick to blame others and cover up our own follies? Welcome back to the garden of Eden!

'The man and his wife were both naked, and they felt no shame' (Genesis 2:25) is the delightful description in the previous chapter of human relationships at their pristine best. Here were people with nothing to hide, nothing to fear and nothing to prove to each other. Pointedly, however, the next three occurrences of the word 'naked' in our reading are all negative. Something had dramatically changed. Their innocence had been replaced by personal insight that was anything but positive. Love and fellowship with God now became guilty fear. Openness, transparency and a clear conscience were superseded by shame that sought to cover up their condition and reluctantly admit, 'I was afraid because I was naked; so I hid.' Hiding from God became their story, and, sadly, it is ours as well.

Guilt and shame, of course, are not popular concepts in

contemporary culture. Undoubtedly, because we are such complex, confused and dysfunctional beings, there are times when we feel shame when we are not guilty and guilt when we have nothing to be ashamed about. Conversely, there are guilty people who feel no shame for their crimes, and shameless people who feel no guilt for their misdemeanours. If we want evidence for the latter assertion, we need only check out the daily tabloids to discover more than enough. And, since there is nothing new under the sun, centuries ago the apostle Paul spoke of those whose 'glory is in their shame' (Philippians 3:19), and elsewhere added that the things done by some people in secret are 'shameful even to mention' (Ephesians 5:12). People are capable of doing the most wonderful things on the one hand, and the most unconscionably wicked on the other.

The guilty couple's attempt at their own 'Watergate' is inevitably a forlorn quest. As we noted yesterday, no one can hide anything from God. Yet, instead of coming clean with God, they preferred to cover up the dirt. Sadly, the divine interrogation only elicits buck-passing, self-justification and due sentence (Genesis 3:8–19). However, even in judgment, the mercy of God can be seen. The couple's flimsy coverings of fig leaves are replaced by something better—'garments of skin' provided by the Lord himself. As many commentators over the centuries have noted, here is both a foretaste of Israel's elaborate sacrificial system and a prophetic pointer to that system's fulfilment in the death of Christ. Ultimately, there on a cross, naked, battered, bruised and dying, Jesus took our guilt and shame and accomplished what animal sacrifices could never achieve: 'to do away with sin by the sacrifice of himself' (Hebrews 9:26). As the prophet Isaiah exuberantly expressed it, 'I delight greatly in the Lord; my soul rejoices in my God. For he has clothed me with garments of salvation and arrayed me in a robe of righteousness' (Isaiah 61:10).

After his resignation from office, when he had eventually 'come clean' about his knowledge of and part in the Watergate scandal, Richard Nixon was issued with a pardon by his successor, Gerald Ford. Centuries earlier, a sage had counselled us: 'He who conceals his sins does not prosper, but whoever confesses and renounces them finds mercy' (Proverbs 28:13). It never pays to cover things up from the omniscient eye of God; it always benefits us to confess our sins. Today, Jesus Christ continues to be God's 'Watergate' for humanity: he is the 'gate' to 'water' that can wash us clean and provide a 'robe of righteousness' that is spotless.

Reflect

Jesus, Thy robe of righteousness
My beauty is, my glorious dress;
'Midst flaming worlds, in this arrayed,
With joy shall I lift up my head.

This spotless robe the same appears,
When ruined nature sinks in years;
No age can change its glorious hue,
The robe of Christ is ever new.
HYMNS OF FAITH 344

COUNT NIKOLAUS LUDWIG VON ZINZENDORF (1739);
TRANS. JOHN WESLEY (1740)

12 December

Alienation

To the woman he said, 'I will greatly increase your pains in childbearing; with pain you will give birth to children. Your desire will be for your husband, and he will rule over you.' To Adam he said, 'Because you listened to your wife and ate from the tree about which I commanded you, "You must not eat of it," Cursed is the ground because of you; through painful toil you will eat of it all the days of your life. It will produce thorns and thistles for you, and you will eat the plants of the field. By the sweat of your brow you will eat your food until you return to the ground, since from it you were taken; for dust you are and to dust you will return.' Adam named his wife Eve, because she would become the mother of all the living. The Lord God made garments of skin for Adam and his wife and clothed them. And the Lord God said, 'The man has now become like one of us, knowing good and evil. He must not be allowed to reach out his hand and take also from the tree of life and eat, and live for ever.' So the Lord God banished him from the Garden of Eden to work the ground from which he had been taken. After he drove the man out, he placed on the east side of the Garden of Eden cherubim and a flaming sword flashing back and forth to guard the way to the tree of life.

Genesis 3:16–24

Therefore remember that at one time you Gentiles in the flesh, called 'the uncircumcision' by what is called the circumcision, which is made in the flesh by hands—remember that you were at that time separated from Christ, alienated from the commonwealth of Israel, and strangers to the covenants of promise, having no hope and without God in the world. But now in Christ Jesus you who once were far off have been brought near by the blood of Christ. For he himself is our peace, who has made us both one and has broken down in his flesh the dividing wall of hostility by abolishing the law of commandments expressed in ordinances, that he might create in himself one new man in place of the two, so making peace, and might reconcile us both to God in one body through the cross, thereby killing the hostility.

Ephesians 2:11–16 (ESV)

In his masterly exposition of Paul's letter to the Ephesians, John Stott observes, '"Alienation" is a popular word in contemporary society.' He then proceeds to link its usage to a household name, Karl Marx (1818–83), and one not so well known, Ludwig Feuerbach (1808–72). Whereas Marx used the word primarily about economics, today, according to Stott, 'the term has become more political than economic. "Alienation" is partly a sense of disaffection with what is, and partly a sense of powerlessness to change it… But long before Feuerbach and Marx the Bible spoke of human alienation',[8] as both our readings today clearly illustrate and remind us.

The scene in Genesis 3 is the human story writ large. The results of disobedience become increasingly apparent. Alienation is a double-edged sword: we discover that we are 'alienated from the commonwealth of Israel' (Ephesians 2:12, ESV)—that is, from other people—and, even more alarmingly, 'alienated from the life of God' (v. 18). The love relationship we were created to have with God has been fractured. What the prophet Isaiah expressed in another context perfectly summaries the scene before us: 'Your iniquities have separated you from your God' (59:2). The result? 'So the Lord God banished him from the Garden of Eden… he drove the man out'. What about alienation from others? Before the couple's disobedience, there was harmony, equality and complementarity between the sexes, as Genesis 2 beautifully illustrates. Now 'Adam named his wife Eve', as he had named the animals, hinting perhaps at the dark dominance he would begin to exercise over her. Meanwhile, Eve discovered, 'Your desire will be for your husband, and he will rule over you'. Whatever else is implied by these statements, the 'war of the sexes' had definitely been engaged. Every pain-filled marriage and every broken relationship finds its taproot here.

Over 40 years ago, Norman Warren published a small evangelistic booklet called *Journey into Life*. It has been the means through which many have found personal faith in Christ, and is still in print and available online. The booklet makes three simple points about 'What sin does': it spoils, spreads and separates. We see this vividly portrayed in the Genesis story. God's world was spoilt, the effects of sin would continue to spread (evidenced by 'thorns and thistles', 3:18), and separation would be the result. Henceforth, human beings have experienced alienation from God, from others, from their environment and, we might add, our very selves: it's little wonder we have identity crises.

Here is humankind, driven from the garden and with no apparent way back to 'the tree of life'. Something in the human heart continues to remind us that we are a long way from home. In a recent interview, Professor Andrew Motion, Poet Laureate from 1999 to 2009 and an atheist who wishes he could believe in God, admitted, 'There's definitely a hole that is God-shaped in my life, no question—and perhaps one day it will get filled.'[9] The Bible's final chapter mentions 'the tree of life' three times.[10] It is a metaphor for the filling of that God-shaped vacuum with the life of God himself. 'The tree of the knowledge of good and evil' caused the human race to stumble; 'the tree of life' can satisfy it.

Our reading from Ephesians reminds us that God has done something to reconcile different types and nationalities of people, like Jews and non-Jews, to himself and one another through another tree that stands between what has been lost and what can be gained. It is called the cross, and it makes possible our homecoming to God and each other. Whenever anyone, of whatever background, nationality, religion or colour, and whatever their personal success or failure, stands at the cross of Jesus, they discover that Calvary is level ground, with no room for pride or position, but lots of space for praise and thanksgiving.

Reflection

When I survey the wondrous cross
On which the Prince of glory died,
My richest gain I count but loss,
And pour contempt on all my pride.

Forbid it, Lord, that I should boast,
Save in the death of Christ my God!
All the vain things that charm me most,
I sacrifice them to His blood.
ISAAC WATTS (1707)

13 December

Death

To Adam he said, 'Because you listened to your wife and ate from the tree about which I commanded you, "You must not eat of it," Cursed is the ground because of you; through painful toil you will eat of it all the days of your life. It will produce thorns and thistles for you, and you will eat the plants of the field. By the sweat of your brow you will eat your food until you return to the ground, since from it you were taken; for dust you are and to dust you will return.'
Genesis 3:17–19

Therefore, just as sin entered the world through one man, and death through sin, and in this way death came to all men, because all sinned—for before the law was given, sin was in the world. But sin is not taken into account when there is no law. Nevertheless, death reigned from the time of Adam to the time of Moses, even over those who did not sin by breaking a command, as did Adam, who was a pattern of the one to come.
Romans 5:12–14

'Statistics show that of those who contract the habit of eating, very few survive' was one of the many humorous observations of George Bernard Shaw (1856–1950), the Irish playwright. He also reputedly said, 'The statistics on death are most impressive: one out of one people die!' But the comedy often surrounding death—gallows' humour, it is sometimes called —should not mask the tragedy and reality of 'the last enemy', as the apostle terms it (1 Corinthians 15:26). These early chapters of Genesis vividly illustrate the point. The permission to eat from any tree save one carried a strict warning: 'for when you eat of it you will surely die' (Genesis 2:17). Eat they did, and die they would. Initially, that death would be 'spiritual'— alienation from God and each other, as we considered yesterday. Eventually, it would be physical.

The ancient Greek philosopher Socrates[11] believed that all philosophy was 'a rumination on death'. The modern German philosopher Martin Heidegger[12] described humanity in terms of a 'Being-toward-death'. The Bible tends to be less philosophically highbrow about death. 'The wages of sin is death' may sound rather blunt (Romans 6:23), but, in the Bible's symphony, it is a major repeating note, though a discordant one. So far as biblical 'philosophy' is concerned, when our forefather sinned he brought death to himself and all his progeny: 'Sin entered into the world through one man, and death through sin' (Romans 5:12). The result is that 'in Adam all die', to quote Paul again (1 Corinthians 15:22).

Genesis 4 and 5 paint a sombre and sobering picture of the human condition: Cain murders Abel (4:8), while violence grows apace as typified by Lamech's boast of killing a young man for an injury inflicted on him (vv. 23–24: an 'honour killing', perhaps, as it might be called today in some circles). Chapter 5, in another context, would be a pension company's nightmare scenario. Do you think Jared had a good innings at 962 years old? Just wait till you meet Methuselah (5:20, 27)! Eight times in that chapter, however, despite the longevity of the men described, we read, '... then he died'.

Some time ago, I was attending a social function at the Metropolitan Police Sports facility in Chigwell, Essex, just a few days before Christmas. 'Xmas Gift,' proclaimed the advert on one of the noticeboards: 'Buy a brick. £20 buys you immortality. Your name will be inscribed forever on the Chigwell plaque, and you will receive a certificate for Christmas. Phone 0208 for details.'

What an offer! Twenty pounds to buy myself immortality! Yet Adam and Eve sold their access to the tree of life for nothing more than a piece of forbidden fruit that cost them a great deal more. And how much would it cost to buy back that access to immortality? Ultimately, it would be a price that no human being could possibly afford. Yet there is a tantalising hint of help and hope even in the 'then he died' narrative of chapter 5: 'Enoch walked with God; then he was no more, because God took him away' (v. 24). Lest we miss the import of that verse, the inspired commentary by the writer to the Hebrews intriguingly states that Enoch 'did not experience death' (11:5). Is that possible? Is there a way through death and into the life of God?

Centuries will roll by; wise men and women, kings and prophets will appear in Israel's history. 'Is this the one who will bring back what our forefather lost?' is an underlying question running through the Bible. Then one day a child appears who will be 'a light for revelation to the Gentiles and for glory to your people Israel', according to Simeon

(Luke 2:32). Years later, the apostle Paul will summarise the situation with theological precision: 'the wages of sin is death' is juxtaposed and contrasted with the astonishing news that 'the gift of God is eternal life in Christ Jesus our Lord' (Romans 6:23).

In a letter written in 1789 to Jean-Baptiste Leroy, Benjamin Franklin observed, 'In this world nothing can be said to be certain, except death and taxes.' Again it is a humorous comment, but, in reality, death is a serious business. More certain, however, is eternal life: Jesus 'has destroyed death and has brought life and immortality to light through the gospel' (2 Timothy 1:10). Rejoice!

Reflect

The grief process, following the loss of someone near and dear, can be overwhelming. Jesus really does understand that. The shortest verse in the King James Version of the Bible is 'Jesus wept' (John 11:35). In that same passage, Jesus says, 'I am the resurrection and the life. He who believes in me will live, even though he dies; and whoever lives and believes in me will never die.' He then adds a question: 'Do you believe this?' (vv. 25–26). Do we? Then we know to whom to take our pain.

14 December

Hope

The man said, 'The woman you put here with me—she gave me some fruit from the tree, and I ate it.' Then the Lord God said to the woman, 'What is this you have done?' The woman said, 'The serpent deceived me, and I ate.' So the Lord God said to the serpent, 'Because you have done this, "Cursed are you above all the livestock and all the wild animals! You will crawl on your belly and you will eat dust all the days of your life. And I will put enmity between you and the woman, and between your offspring and hers; he will crush your head, and you will strike his heel."'
Genesis 3:12–15

'Ferry 'cross the Mersey' was a 1960s hit written by Gerry Marsden and performed by him and his band The Pacemakers. We loved it in Liverpool, for, times without number, many of us had taken that ferry ride. Having crossed the Mersey, the boat would approach the floating landing stage and a thin rope would be thrown to a man standing on it. As he hauled the rope towards himself, it began to pull behind it the huge thick ropes that would be used to moor the ferry and secure it to the wharf. In similar fashion, the statement that God intends to put enmity between the serpent and the woman, and between its offspring and hers, may seem like a rather 'thin rope'; but, as it is tugged, it wonderfully pulls all the major strands of the Bible's story with it. Eventually, what we could call the 'ferry of deliverance', from the other side of the river, arrives in a backwater of planet earth. 'It will ultimately transport countless passengers back to the place from which it came. However, it won't be plain sailing: 'enmity', 'crushing of heads' and 'striking of heels' all ensure that there will be many storms to be faced and circumnavigated if the ferry is to accomplish its task. This is a major part of The Incredible Journey.

We may wish it otherwise, but the 'storm warning' is clear. The purposes of God will be opposed on planet earth at every turn. Henceforth, conflict there will be. God's kingdom—that is, his rule in the here and now, to be consummated later—will be contested. 'The world, the flesh and the devil' is a helpful summary of the state of affairs: I face challenges from outside myself, within myself, and beyond myself and my visible world. Seen through that lens, the Old Testament story of 'Detouring often', which we will consider in more detail in next week's readings, comes into sharp focus. Advances and retreats, victories and defeats, heroes and villains, saints and sinners, triumphs and disasters will be the evidence of it. This will be no less true when the 'ferry of deliverance' arrives: Christ's coming summoned enemy engagement long before it culminated in his cross.[13]

In verse 15 of today's reading, the Revised Standard Version helpfully retains the King James Version's word 'seed' in preference to NIV's 'offspring': 'enmity… between your seed and her seed'. It is a loaded word theologically. Seth became the bearer of the seed's promise after Abel's death;

Abram's seed would be as countless as the stars; David's seed would be established and endure for ever; when all seemed hopeless, a 'holy seed' would survive, according to Isaiah.[14] Where is all this headed? What does it portend? Centuries later, while preaching in Pisidian Antioch, Paul reminded his hearers that from King David's seed 'God has brought to Israel the Saviour Jesus', pointedly adding, 'as he promised' (Acts 13:23). Where did God promise that? Here in Genesis 3:15, millennia before!

The final part of the promise, after all the storms have ceased, envisages a safe haven when the 'seed' finally 'will bruise' the serpent's head (Genesis 3:15, ESV). Paul echoes that promise in his letter to the Romans: 'The God of peace will soon crush Satan under your feet' (16:20). Christ, not Satan, will triumph at the last.

On 25 May 1961, President John F. Kennedy announced an ambitious and audacious goal: before the end of that decade, America would commit itself to 'landing a man on the moon and returning him safely to the Earth'.[15] On 20 July 1969, the Apollo space flight duly landed Commander Neil Armstrong and lunar module pilot Buzz Aldrin on the moon's Sea of Tranquillity: 'That's one small step for a man, a giant leap for mankind', were Neil Armstrong's near-immortal words. Less spectacularly to the human eye, but to the heavens' awed amazement, Genesis 3:15 is God's stupendous announcement of his intention to send a Saviour not to a sea of tranquillity but to an ocean of trouble. There's a ferry across the oceans of time, and a 'shuttle' across the ravages of space, which brings us home to God. Thank God for Jesus.

Reflection

If our greatest need had been information,
God would have sent us an educator.

If our greatest need had been technology,
God would have sent us a scientist.

If our greatest need had been money,
God would have sent us an economist.

If our greatest need had been pleasure,
God would have sent us an entertainer.

But our greatest was forgiveness,
So God sent us a Saviour.[16]

NOTES

1   E.J. Young, *In the Beginning* (Banner of Truth, 1976), p. 90.
2   From 'The Weight of Glory' in Lesley Walmsley (ed.), *C.S. Lewis Essay Collection & Other Short Pieces* (Fount, 2000), pp. 98–99.
3   See 1 Timothy 3:6 and Ezekiel 28, especially vv. 5, 12–13.
4   John 13:7.
5   C.H. Spurgeon, *Morning and Evening*, revised and updated by Alistair Begg (Crossway Books, 2003), from reading for the evening of 5 September.
6   David Atkinson, *The Message of Genesis 1—11* (IVP, 1990), p. 90.
7   Giorgio Armani, 'What I've learnt', *The Times Magazine* (18 September 2010), p. 8.
8   John R.W. Stott, *God's New Society* (IVP, 1979), p. 89.
9   *Third Way* (April 2009), p. 20.
10 Revelation 22:2, 14, 19.
11 469–399BC.
12 1889–1976.
13 See, for instance, Matthew 2:13–18; 4:1–11.
14 See Genesis 4:25; 15:5; Psalm 89:4, 29; Isaiah 6:13.
15 Richard Stenger, 'Man on the moon: Kennedy speech ignited the dream', posted 25 May 2001 at www.CNN.com/space; accessed 19 August 2010.
16 From a Christmas card produced by DaySpring Cards: www.dayspring.com.

15–21 December

DETOURING OFTEN

*The Old Testament stands in discontinuity with the New because it
speaks a BC word, not an AD word. But this very fact gives it an
amazing continuity with BC man: it can speak to his condition…*

*This BC perspective of the Old Testament is the essential complement
to the AD perspective of the New. Because of its very humanity, and
because it drives ahead towards a future it never attains, the Old
Testament raises questions, poses problems which every sensitive reader
sees are his own problems, the problems of the world and of all mankind.
And just because it involves BC man in the problems, yet can give to
them no final solution, it impels him toward some better solution—
beyond the limits of BC…*

*The Old Testament's word therefore mirrors even before him
the predicament that, but for Christ, besets him,
and impels him anew to the gospel.*

JOHN BRIGHT[1]

15 December

Abraham: a father

By faith Abraham, when called to go to a place he would later receive as his inheritance, obeyed and went, even though he did not know where he was going. By faith he made his home in the promised land like a stranger in a foreign country; he lived in tents, as did Isaac and Jacob, who were heirs with him of the same promise. For he was looking forward to the city with foundations, whose architect and builder is God. By faith Abraham, even though he was past age—and Sarah herself was barren—was enabled to become a father because he considered him faithful who had made the promise. And so from this one man, and he as good as dead, came descendants as numerous as the stars in the sky and as countless as the sand on the seashore. All these people were still living by faith when they died. They did not receive the things promised; they only saw them and welcomed them from a distance. And they admitted that they were aliens and strangers on earth. People who say such things show that they are looking for a country of their own. If they had been thinking of the country they had left, they would have had opportunity to return. Instead, they were longing for a better country—a heavenly one. Therefore God is not ashamed to be called their God, for he has prepared a city for them. By faith Abraham, when God tested him, offered Isaac as a sacrifice. He who had received the promises was about to sacrifice his one and only son, even though God had said to him, 'It is through Isaac that your offspring will be reckoned.' Abraham reasoned that God could raise the dead, and figuratively speaking, he did receive Isaac back from death.

Hebrews 11:8–19

There's no dodging Abraham! In our world, he is claimed as the father of the three great monotheistic faiths of Judaism, Christianity and Islam. Biblically, he is an immense character, being mentioned nearly 300 times. His journeys around the ancient world have drawn comparisons with Christopher Columbus' voyages to the New World of America: at times, like Abraham, Columbus 'did not know where he was going' either! In Abraham's case, however, a whole new world would be discovered that would dwarf the achievements of Columbus. To billions of people a new world of faith in the living God would be opened up, a spiritual universe of infinite possibilities secured by Jesus Christ.

The writer to the Hebrews highlights for us some of Abraham's rip-roaring life of faith. When he was called to go, the writer comments tersely, he 'obeyed and went'. It is easy to overlook the initial faith that moved him out of his comfort zone. God had told him to 'leave your country, your people and your father's household', bidding farewell to the city of 'Ur of the Chaldeans' (Genesis 12:1; 11:31). At that period, around 2000BC, Ur was a prominent, highly developed city, enjoying both peace and prosperity. It was also idolatrous, its temple precincts boasting a ziggurat dedicated to Nanna, the moon god. However, 'saving faith' inevitably involves turning to God from idols—whether they be the metal ones of ancient civilisations or the mental ones of the modern urban sophisticate ('I prefer to think of God like this...'). The result is that we are then free 'to serve the living and true God' (1 Thessalonians 1:9). Sometimes, such repentance demands that a person make a dramatic change of location and vocation, like one of our Moorlands students who used to be a male stripper, or another who is 'dead meat' if his previous life catches up with him.

The life of faith can be really exhilarating. Abraham was prepared to live as a stranger in a foreign country—to rough it, we might say, living in tents and never giving up on the hope of finding a 'city with foundations, whose architect and builder is God'. That same faith gifted him with a long-awaited promised son, Isaac, even when he was 100 years old. It also gave him courage to be prepared to return this gift when God mysteriously seemed to require Isaac as a sacrifice, for he believed in God's ability to raise the dead (note Hebrews 11:11, 17 and 19 especially).

But there's a flipside to Abraham's seemingly abundant life of faith. The 'highlights' in Hebrews are counterbalanced by the low points that Genesis painstakingly records. Not once but twice he lied about his relationship to his wife, putting her in a compromised position, and both of them in real danger. Another time, at his wife's insistence, he created his own providence with regard to an heir, sleeping with Sarah's maidservant, Hagar, and producing a son, Ishmael. Later, he would be emotionally torn apart by the consequences of that bad decision, when he had to send the boy Ishmael away, and he created tensions in his immediate and wider family for centuries to come.[2]

So, just as in our own experience, Abraham's faith was, at times, a mixed bag, trusting God for the big things and stumbling over smaller challenges. The reason why he is commended, however, is that he never let go of the promise that God would make him into a great nation in order to bless 'all peoples on earth' (Genesis 12:2–3). How? God's *modus operandi* would be through Abraham's 'offspring' or 'seed'. That recurring theme, as we noted yesterday, links back to Genesis and is stitched into the fabric of the unfolding story of the Old Testament.[3] Its fulfilment would be found, according to the New Testament, in the coming of Jesus Christ, who is both 'of the seed of David' and 'the seed of Abraham' (2 Timothy 2:8; Hebrews 2:16, KJV). In a compact argument in Galatians, Paul's conclusion is that when we belong to Jesus Christ, we too spiritually become 'Abraham's seed, and heirs according to the promise' (Galatians 3:29).[4] Whatever my background, whatever my ups and downs of faith, through Jesus Christ I am rooted into Abraham's family and become a person of destiny—an heir. Small wonder that Abraham, according to Jesus, rejoiced at the thought of seeing Christ's day: 'he saw it and was glad' (John 8:56). Aren't you?

Reflect

For some of us, the low points of Abraham's faith seem strangely more encouraging than the highlights. Is that a good or bad thing?

16 December

Joseph: a saviour

When Jacob learned that there was grain in Egypt, he said to his sons, 'Why do you just keep looking at each other?' He continued, 'I have heard that there is grain in Egypt. Go down there and buy some for us, so that we may live and not die.' Then ten of Joseph's brothers went down to buy grain from Egypt. But Jacob did not send Benjamin, Joseph's brother, with the others, because he was afraid that harm might come to him...

As soon as Joseph saw his brothers, he recognised them, but he pretended to be a stranger and spoke harshly to them. 'Where do you come from?' he asked. 'From the land of Canaan,' they replied, 'to buy food.' Although Joseph recognised his brothers, they did not recognise him. Then he remembered his dreams about them and said to them, 'You are spies! You have come to see where our land is unprotected.' 'No, my lord,' they answered. 'Your servants have come to buy food.' ...

On the third day, Joseph said to them, 'Do this and you will live, for I fear God: If you are honest men, let one of your brothers stay here in prison, while the rest of you go and take grain back for your starving households. But you must bring your youngest brother to me, so that your words may be verified and that you may not die.' This they proceeded to do. They said to one another, 'Surely we are being punished because of our brother. We saw how distressed he was when he pleaded with us for his life, but we would not listen; that's why this distress has come upon us.' Reuben replied, 'Didn't I tell you not to sin against the boy? But you wouldn't listen! Now we must give an accounting for his blood.' They did not realise that Joseph could understand them, since he was using an interpreter. He turned away from them and began to weep, but then turned back and spoke to them again. He had Simeon taken from them and bound before their eyes.

Genesis 42:1–4, 7–10, 18–24

The Joseph we normally associate with Christmas is not the one whose fame has spawned the Rice/Lloyd Webber musical, *Joseph and the Amazing Technicolor Dreamcoat*. Nevertheless, we discover that he too is integral to the Christmas story.

'God spoke to our forefathers... at many times and in various ways', the writer to the Hebrews reminds us (1:1). Sometimes, for example, God's revelation came as direct commands, such as the Ten Commandments. At other times, narrative, parables and proverbs were used that made people stop, think and mull things over. Accordingly, half the book of Genesis is utilised to paint a multicoloured picture on a large narrative canvas to deal with two main characters—Jacob and his favoured son, Joseph. At one level, it is appropriate to read these chapters and draw moral and spiritual lessons on families, their brokenness and healing, and their various heroes and villains (and there are plenty of the latter). However, their main purpose is not to excite our disapproval or admiration. Primarily, they are the story of God himself and his dealings in sheer grace with Abraham's offspring.

Most Christians have heard of the exodus—the Israelites' leaving of Egypt. Intriguingly, these chapters introduce us to the question of how Israel came to be in Egypt in the first place. What was the context for an ancient patriarchal family's relocation from what they thought was their promised homeland of Canaan to Egypt? The narrative supplies its shocking and appalling answers: family intrigues, deceit, double-dealing, murder, rape, adultery, prostitution, narrowly aborted fratricide, cover-ups and more. If this small bunch of nomads were ever to be guardians of the purposes of God, bearers of the seed of Abraham and ultimately the ancestors of the Jewish race, destined to be 'a light for the Gentiles' (Isaiah 49:6), then special and desperate measures would be necessary. In Egypt, they would be almost hermetically sealed off from Canaan's pagan influences, given their own territory in the land of Goshen and enabled to grow, without too much Egyptian interference, into a great multitude of a nation.[5] For that to happen, a special envoy was necessary. Enter Joseph.

Nearly 40 years ago, I heard a young preacher friend memorably sum up the trajectory of Joseph's life as 'from pit to prison to palace'. In our reading today, we are introduced to him in the palace phase of his life. When he was governor of Egypt, most of his brothers turned up unexpectedly, brought there by famine. Have you ever had the experience, years on, of coming across someone who bullied you in childhood? When I did, I was surprised at how small and vulnerable he appeared, when he had seemed to tower over me when I was a youngster. Over 20 years have elapsed since the shocking events recorded in Genesis 37, when Joseph's brothers sold him into slavery. Now the tables have been dramatically turned. Will Joseph take the opportunity to get even with his abusers?

At one level, there is something farcical about the games Joseph proceeds to play in this and subsequent chapters: who has ever heard of a group of ten spies—brothers, at that? But his purpose is totally serious. Are there any signs of repentance for what they did, or has their self-justification continued over those long years, along the lines of 'He had it coming to him for all that "family favourite" treatment he got from the old man, for being a snitch and parading around in that special coat'? Has there been any change in them? That is what Joseph needs to know—for, without change, reconciliation in families or to God is impossible. Clearly, however, there have been stirrings in their hearts. Conscience can gnaw away at people year after year about their 'skeletons in the cupboard', as verses 21 and 22 graphically illustrate.

At this point in the narrative, Joseph is presented as an unrecognised saviour. The one his brothers thought 'no more' (42:13) was in fact alive, listening to their conversation, moved to tears and in a position to become their saviour and provider throughout the famine and beyond. When you are 'ruler of all Egypt' (45:8), you can do things like that. Accordingly, Joseph acts as a type—that is, a pattern of someone else.

In summary, we note that Joseph was loved by his father as a special son, but rejected by his brothers. He suffered unjustly for no crime he had committed and was presumed dead, yet was wonderfully alive. He was exalted to a throne and became the saviour of his people. Does that remind you of anyone? 'You are to give him the name Jesus, because he will save his people from their sins' (Matthew 1:21).

Reflection

Has your family life or wider network of friendships been marked by abuse and unbelief? Perhaps, with one or two friends, it is time to 'pray for those who ill-treat you' (Luke 6:28) and ask the unrecognised Saviour to meet them in mercy, too.

17 December

Moses: a law giver

And God spoke all these words: 'I am the Lord your God, who brought you out of Egypt, out of the land of slavery. You shall have no other gods before me. You shall not make for yourself an idol in the form of anything in heaven above or on the earth beneath or in the waters below. You shall not bow down to them or worship them; for I, the Lord your God, am a jealous God, punishing the children for the sin of the fathers to the third and fourth generation of those who hate me, but showing love to a thousand generations of those who love me and keep my commandments. You shall not misuse the name of the Lord your God, for the Lord will not hold anyone guiltless who misuses his name. Remember the Sabbath day by keeping it holy. Six days you shall labour and do all your work, but the seventh day is a Sabbath to the Lord your God. On it you shall not do any work, neither you, nor your son or daughter, nor your manservant or maidservant, nor your animals, nor the alien within your gates. For in six days the Lord made the heavens and the earth, the sea, and all that is in them, but he rested on the seventh day. Therefore the Lord blessed the Sabbath day and made it holy. Honour your father and your mother, so that you may live long in the land the Lord your God is giving you. You shall not murder. You shall not commit adultery.

You shall not steal. You shall not give false testimony against your neighbour. You shall not covet your neighbour's house. You shall not covet your neighbour's wife, or his manservant or maidservant, his ox or donkey, or anything that belongs to your neighbour.'
Exodus 20:1–17

Lawman was one of Warner Brothers' Westerns, screened regularly from 1958 to 1962. It starred John Russell as Marshall Dan Troop, the upright, uncompromised upholder of the law in the Wild West of Laramie City, Wyoming. It was a straightforward Western, with occasional lighter moments and little time for romance, but a dogged determination to sort out the 'bad guys'.

Unlike Marshall Troop, however, Moses himself had been on the wrong side of the law. Exodus 2 tells how he was forced to flee his privileged position in the Egyptian court after he killed an Egyptian who was beating one of his fellow Hebrews. The next phase of his life was in stark contrast to his first 40 years of privilege. Having fled to Midian, he found a welcome, a wife and seeming obscurity, but the promises of God were still being worked out, and they were going to involve him. The Lord 'remembered his covenant… looked on the Israelites and was concerned about them', for he had heard 'their cry for help' (Exodus 2:23–25). The rest of the Exodus story—the burning bush, the plagues on Egypt, the Passover, the escape from Egypt, the crossing of the Red Sea and the giving of the law—would flow out of that divine concern and compassion. For his final 40 years, Moses would be integral to God's rescue plan.

So, in summary, Moses' life divided neatly into three equal parts. Brought up as a royal prince, for 40 years he was a somebody. Then he made a huge mistake and became a no-body for the next 40. Finally, in the last stage of life, he was a something for God, making an incalculable contribution to Israel and leaving a lasting legacy to the wider world—the very mind of the Creator expressed in the law of God.

Before examining those stages a little further, it may be helpful to pause and consider our own lives. Some of us may have been born into privilege, but many of us were not. Some of us may have made catastrophic midlife choices, while others have just jogged cheerfully through midlife crisis. Yet, for Moses, subdued by God's grace, the latter part of his life proved to be the most significant stage. How and where we finish is usually far more important than where we came from or how we started.

The rabbis calculated that there were 613 different laws in the Pentateuch (the first five books of our Bible): 365 'don'ts' and 248 'dos'. The Ten Commandments are a summary of Israel's wider legislation, four commands emphasising our relationship with God, and six our relationship with our neighbours. Jesus masterfully summarised the whole law into just two commands: 'Love the Lord your God... [and] love your neighbour as yourself' (Mark 12:30–31).

As a rule for living, the law is marvellous according to the psalmist: 'O, how I love your law! I meditate on it all day long' (Psalm 119:97). There's nothing wrong with the law of God in general or the Ten Commandments in particular. They portray the character of God as holy, enumerate his standards and help to restrain evil in the world. The opposite of the law is not freedom but anarchy. Accordingly, the apostle Paul affirmed that 'the law is holy, and the commandment is holy, righteous and good' (Romans 7:12).

But herein lies the problem that the Bible continually addresses. 'The law is spiritual', the apostle adds, and then focuses the issue: 'but I am unspiritual, sold as a slave to sin… Who will rescue me…?' (vv. 14, 24). When I look in a mirror, I expect to see myself. If my face is dirty and my hair unkempt, the mirror can reveal my condition, but it cannot remove the dirt or comb my hair. A few verses later in Romans, Paul provides an answer to his rhetorical question: 'What the law was powerless to do in that it was weakened by the sinful nature, God did by sending his own Son' (8:3). Indeed, the New Testament story adds that 'the law was put in charge to lead us to Christ that we might be justified by faith' (Galatians 3:24). Reading the book of Exodus and all the laws of God from this side of the coming of Jesus, the pregnant phrase 'I have come down to rescue them' (Exodus 3:8) finds ultimate fulfilment in the one who, though God, 'became flesh and made his dwelling among us' that first Christmas. If 'the law was given by Moses, grace and truth came through Jesus Christ', because of the God who 'so loved the world' that he gave him for us (John 1:14, 18; 3:16). Take time to stop, wonder and worship.

Reflection

'Morality cannot be legislated but behaviour can be regulated. Judicial decrees may not change hearts but they can restrict the heartless' (Dr Martin Luther King).[6] *Would you agree?*

18 December

Joshua: a leader

After the death of Moses the servant of the Lord, the Lord said to Joshua son of Nun, Moses' assistant: 'Moses my servant is dead. Now then, you and all these people, get ready to cross the Jordan River into the land I am about to give to them—to the Israelites. I will give you every place where you set your foot, as I promised Moses. Your territory will extend from the desert to Lebanon, and from the great river, the Euphrates—all the Hittite country—to the Great Sea on the west. No-one will be able to stand up against you all the days of your life. As I was with Moses, so I will be with you; I will never leave you nor forsake you. Be strong and courageous, because you will lead these people to inherit the land I swore to their forefathers to give them. Be strong and very courageous. Be careful to obey all the law my servant Moses gave you; do not turn from it to the right or to the left, that you may be successful wherever you go. Do not let this Book of the Law depart from your mouth; meditate on it day and night, so that you may be careful to do everything written in it. Then you will be prosperous and successful. Have I not commanded you? Be strong and courageous. Do not be terrified; do not be discouraged, for the Lord your God will be with you wherever you go.'

Joshua 1:1–9

When Joshua was old and well advanced in years, the Lord said to him, 'You are very old, and there are still very large areas of land to be taken over.'
Joshua 13:1

'They clearly did not like the church, its music or me,' is how my pastor friend described the situation. He was referring to a couple who had recently left his congregation. It turned out subsequently that they had hopped around a number of other churches expressing similar dislikes about various things. My friend never appeared to be the type who is over-sensitive to criticism. (That in itself is unusual for pastors: their hearts bleed with the best and wound more easily than they often care to admit—at least in my observations from the hundreds I know.) But one day the proverbial final straw was added to this pastorally willing camel's back. It occurred during a series of studies in the book of Joshua. The couple in question turned on him: how could he possibly be making so many applications to Christians from that book? Before he knew it, he'd unloaded both barrels of months of frustration: 'So, seeing as you know so much about the book of Joshua,' he said, 'perhaps you'd give me your take on its eschatological purpose!' Answers on a postcard to...! The couple left the church shortly thereafter

His riposte was not entirely facetious. There is an eschatological purpose at work here. Appropriately, the rabbis dubbed the section of books to which Joshua belongs 'The Former Prophets', so it has both an immediate and a prophetic application. Firstly, it is the story of the conquest of the land of Canaan. When he was old, even after he had fought so well and accomplished so much, Joshua was reminded by the Lord that 'there are still very large areas of land to be taken over'. Like 'seed' in our previous readings, 'land/earth' is a much-used word, occurring over 2500 times in the Old Testament. The God who originally made the 'earth' also promised a 'land' to Abraham. Its initial acquisition (as here in Joshua), its later subjugation by Babylonian invaders, and its restoration, following Cyrus' decree after 70 years of the people's captivity, is a major theme of Old Testament history.[7] Psalm 37 alone has some half dozen references to the land and the kind of people who would inherit it. The last Old Testament book in our Bibles, Malachi, foresees a day when Canaan once again will be 'a delightful land' (3:12), echoing Isaiah's vision of an earth 'full of the knowledge of the Lord as the waters cover the sea', and freed from its tyranny, barbarity and injustices (Isaiah 11:1–9).

The theme is continued as the New Testament opens. Something is astir in the 'land' of Judah. A ruler-shepherd arises from Bethlehem. In his teaching he promises that people like the meek, not the power-hungry, will be the ones to inherit the 'earth/land'. But the cost will involve darkness 'over the land' when the Teacher's cross is lifted high and he tastes 'God-forsakenness' for those he has come to save. Soon, however, once risen from the dead, he claims all authority in heaven and on 'earth', and commissions his followers to take his gospel to all peoples everywhere.[8] How are they to accomplish such a seemingly overwhelming task?

Back in the book of Joshua, we note the ups and downs, the victories and failures of Israel as she claims the 'promised land'. Miraculous interventions, incredible progress and gut-wrenching betrayal are all documented. (Check out chapters 3, 6 and 7 for a start.) There is no straight and uncomplicated path towards establishing God's kingdom on earth. Similarly, when we turn to the Church's history book, Acts, we are confronted by similar ups and downs: the coming of the promised Holy Spirit, astonishing miracles, rapid growth and deep personal failure and hypocrisy, all in the first five chapters. But the gospel continues to spread around the Roman Empire, touching the very centre of imperial power as Paul reaches Rome (Acts 28:14). How did the believers keep going, in spite of all the opposition encountered along the way? At one level the answer seems simplistic: those early Christians relied on the power of the Holy Spirit to enable them to keep proclaiming and living the gospel of God's grace in Christ.

Does the foregoing story of the Church seem a million miles away from the book of Joshua? It shouldn't. Joshua means 'Yahweh saves/rescues'. Its New Testament equivalent is, of course, 'Jesus'. Unlike his namesake, and without shedding any blood but his own, he still calls all sorts of people to his promised land—'a new heaven and a new earth, the home of righteousness' (2 Peter 3:13), using Christians like us as pointers to him and his kingdom. Now that really is eschatological!

Reflection

He did not come to judge the world,
He did not come to blame;
He did not only come to seek,
It was to save he came.

And when we call him Saviour,
And when we call him Saviour,
And when we call him Saviour,
Then we call him by his Name.
ANON

19 December

David: a shepherd-king

The Lord said to Samuel, 'How long will you mourn for Saul, since I have rejected him as king over Israel? Fill your horn with oil and be on your way; I am sending you to Jesse of Bethlehem. I have chosen one of his sons to be king.' But Samuel said, 'How can I go? Saul will hear about it and kill me.' The Lord said, 'Take a heifer with you and say, "I have come to sacrifice to the Lord." Invite Jesse to the sacrifice, and I will show you what to do. You are to anoint for me the one I indicate.' Samuel did what the Lord said. When he arrived at Bethlehem, the elders of the town trembled when they met him. They asked, 'Do you come in peace?' Samuel replied, 'Yes, in peace; I have come to sacrifice to the Lord. Consecrate yourselves and come to the sacrifice with me.' Then he consecrated Jesse and his sons and invited them to the sacrifice. When they arrived, Samuel saw Eliab and thought, Surely the Lord's anointed stands here before the Lord. But the Lord said to Samuel, 'Do not consider his appearance or his height, for I have rejected him. The Lord does not look at the things man looks at. Man looks at the outward appearance, but the Lord looks at the heart.' Then Jesse called Abinadab and made him pass in front of Samuel. But Samuel said, 'The Lord has not chosen this one either.'

Jesse then made Shammah pass by, but Samuel said, 'Nor has the Lord chosen this one.' Jesse made seven of his sons pass before Samuel, but Samuel said to him, 'The Lord has not chosen these.' So he asked Jesse, 'Are these all the sons you have?' 'There is still the youngest,' Jesse answered, 'but he is tending the sheep.' Samuel said, 'Send for him; we will not sit down until he arrives.' So he sent and had him brought in. He was ruddy, with a fine appearance and handsome features. Then the Lord said, 'Rise and anoint him; he is the one.' So Samuel took the horn of oil and anointed him in the presence of his brothers, and from that day on the Spirit of the Lord came upon David in power. Samuel then went to Ramah.

1 Samuel 16:1–13

'Be careful what you wish for' would be one way to summarise ancient Israel's desire to be like their neighbours and have a king. Saul was duly anointed (see 1 Samuel 8 and 9), but, after a honeymoon period, like a wife who realises that the man she has married is a violent alcoholic, Israel discovered that her king was a paranoid tyrant, self-willed and disobedient. Over the following 500 years of Israel's monarchy, Saul would have many imitators—and, if we look around our world today, clearly he has many successors.

The Lord then 'sought out a man after his own heart', the earlier narrative records (1 Samuel 13:14). The prophet Samuel is duly despatched and is warned not to judge the replacement king by outward appearance, since 'the Lord looks at the heart'. The new king is not discovered as a prince in a palace but as a fresh-faced youth, tending sheep as part of the family business. 'Rise and anoint him; he is the one,' Samuel is instructed when David appears. The remaining chapters of 1 Samuel record David's struggles and problems with Saul, while the second book of Samuel could easily be retitled 'the second book of David', for he is its main character. Although eclipsed in outward splendour by Solomon his son, no king dominates the Old Testament's narrative like David. All together, he is mentioned over 1000 times in the Bible. His exploits were fabulous, his faith strong, his kingdom increasingly secure and his failure legendary. Failure? Like Saul before him, and every king and pretender after him, he had shortcomings and the Bible does not glaze over them. He too had feet of clay.

Even a cursory reading of 2 Samuel is salutary. The first ten chapters record David's victories, chapters 11 and 12 his personal failure with another man's wife, Bathsheba, and the final dozen chapters mainly his defeats and mounting problems. The man who wrote the most famous of all the psalms, 'The Lord is my shepherd' (Psalm 23), also penned the greatest psalm of repentance, following on from the discovery of his adultery: 'Have mercy on me, O God… wash me, and I will be whiter than snow… Create in me a pure heart, O God' (51:1, 7, 10). Like so many of us, David was a mixture of triumphs and disasters in the realm of faith.

For me, it is an immense privilege to be involved at Moorlands College in training a new generation of Christian workers, some of whom are spectacularly gifted even before their training. However, there is a maxim I regularly quote at myself and to others: 'Charisma without character may lead to catastrophe.' David was immensely charismatic, endowed with superlative gifts. His character generally was good, forged by the warmth of a good family and in the white heat of conflict, disappointment and life as a fugitive running from Saul. But in his case, there were character flaws—his weakness for women among other things—that eventually led to his committing adultery and murder. We all need to be reminded regularly that a reputation that has taken 30 years to build may be smashed into a thousand pieces by ten minutes of stupidity and recklessness. In David's case, in the mercy of God, complete catastrophe did not follow his folly, but chaos was introduced into his family's life. Seduction and incestuous rape, fratricide, conspiracies and revolts are all recorded in the latter half of 2 Samuel. With a family like David's, who'd need enemies?

The most remarkable part of David's story, however, was yet to be written. Through 'the house and line of David' (Luke 2:4), notwithstanding all its chequered history, God intended to send the Shepherd-King. What really is so amazing about God's grace is that it tolerates the weakness of human nature in order to redeem it. That's one reason why the wise or the foolish, when they come to the shepherd who gave his life for his erring sheep, 'bow down and worship' the king of grace (Matthew 2:11).

Reflection

Hail to the Lord's anointed,
Great David's greater Son!
Hail, in the time appointed,
His reign on earth begun!

He comes to break oppression,
To set the captive free;
To take away transgression,
And rule in equity.
JAMES MONTGOMERY (1821)

20 December

Isaiah: a servant

See, my servant will act wisely; he will be raised and lifted up and highly exalted. Just as there were many who were appalled at him—his appearance was so disfigured beyond that of any man and his form marred beyond human likeness—so will he sprinkle many nations, and kings will shut their mouths because of him. For what they were not told, they will see, and what they have not heard, they will understand.

Who has believed our message and to whom has the arm of the Lord been revealed? He grew up before him like a tender shoot, and like a root out of dry ground. He had no beauty or majesty to attract us to him, nothing in his appearance that we should desire him. He was despised and rejected by men, a man of sorrows, and familiar with suffering. Like one from whom men hide their faces he was despised, and we esteemed him not.

Surely he took up our infirmities and carried our sorrows, yet we considered him stricken by God, smitten by him, and afflicted. But he was pierced for our transgressions, he was crushed for our iniquities; the punishment that brought us peace was upon him, and by his wounds we are healed. We all, like sheep, have gone astray, each of us has turned to his own way; and the Lord has laid on him the iniquity of us all.

He was oppressed and afflicted, yet he did not open his mouth; he was led like a lamb to the slaughter, and as a sheep before her shearers is silent, so he did not open his mouth. By oppression and judgment he was taken away. And who can speak of his descendants? For he was cut off from the land of the living; for the transgression of my people he was stricken. He was assigned a grave with the wicked, and with the rich in his death, though he had done no violence, nor was any deceit in his mouth.

Yet it was the Lord's will to crush him and cause him to suffer, and though the Lord makes his life a guilt offering, he will see his offspring and prolong his days, and the will of the Lord will prosper in his hand. After the suffering of his soul, he will see the light of life and be satisfied; by his knowledge my righteous servant will justify many, and he will bear their iniquities. Therefore I will give him a portion among the great, and he will divide the spoils with the strong, because he poured out his life unto death, and was numbered with the transgressors. For he bore the sin of many, and made intercession for the transgressors.

Isaiah 52:13—53:12

The eighth-century prophecy of Isaiah contains the unfathomable depths and momentous heights of what are termed 'the servant songs'. They introduce us to a chosen one, the Lord's anointed, loved and honoured by God, yet amazingly despised and rejected by his own people. Nevertheless, he never deviates from his mission to rescue, help and save. This final one of the four traditional 'songs of the servant' is the best-known. It is quoted and echoed repeatedly in the New Testament. It is composed of five stanzas:

- The Saviour of the World (52:13–15)
- The Man of Sorrows (53:1–3)
- The Burden Bearer (53:4–6)
- The Lamb of God (53:7–9)
- The Risen Lord (53:10–12)

The first stanza acts as an overview of the servant's vocation. Highest exaltation is counter-balanced with unimaginable depths of suffering and human disfigurement, which result in his cleansing or 'sprinkling' many nations, not merely his own people. The second section records the servant's inconspicuous and unpromising beginnings, 'like a root out of dry ground' with no outward marks of majesty or brilliance to set him apart from the crowd. Indeed, his outstanding feature would be the utter rejection he experienced, rendering him 'a man of sorrows', eschewed by all. 'Who could have believed what we have heard?' asks the astonished prophet (53:1, REB). It's as if he 'came to his own, and his own people did not receive him', to anticipate the New Testament's perspective (John 1:11, ESV). The song's central verses paint a graphically dark picture of humanity's condition and its need: 'infirmities… sorrows… transgressions… iniquities… gone astray… turned to [its] own way'. The interplay of 'our/us/we' with 'his/him/he' is striking. The servant undergoes extreme violence, being 'pierced' and 'crushed'—terms expressing the excruciatingly painful nature of his death. The witnesses realise that they themselves deserved those sufferings, but that the servant has taken their place. As Barry Webb comments, 'Substitution was not a new thought to the Israelites; it was enshrined in the law of Moses... now the witnesses see that this same principle is at work in the suffering and death of the Servant.'[9]

That ancient law of God had previously introduced Israel to various sacrificial offerings, none more memorable than the Passover lamb (Exodus 12). In the song's fourth part, suffering in lamb-like silence, the servant is 'cut off from the land of the living' for his people's transgressions, though he is guilty of neither violence nor deceit. Normally, the shocking death of such a 'malefactor' would be enough to have his remains consigned to an ignominious grave. Amazingly, however, it is 'with the rich' that his corpse finds its lodging.

The final instalment is a grand crescendo, heralding the triumph of the vilified. His death was part of the divine plan that ensured that the 'guilt offering' of himself (see Leviticus 5:5) was precisely 'enough' to put the 'many' right with God.

The word 'therefore' in the final verse of today's reading is crucial. The servant's degradation, humiliation and death are vindicated by God's turning the tables of human judgment. Amazingly and appropriately, the pierced, crushed, bruised, dead and buried sufferer is raised to life and 'highly exalted'. Now this servant will enjoy the fruits of his suffering: 'I will apportion to him the many' is the illuminating translation from Alec Motyer.[10] This servant will have a people of his own, ultimately a forgiven and restored humanity under his care and sway.

Centuries after the prophecy was uttered, a high-ranking Ethiopian official was reading this passage when the early

Christian evangelist, Philip, joined him on the road. 'Tell me, please, who is the prophet talking about, himself or someone else?' the Ethiopian asked. The book of Acts records that Philip 'began with that very passage of Scripture and told him the good news about Jesus' (Acts 8:34–35). Isaiah's question still echoes down the ages: 'Who has believed our message?' Your church? Your family? You?

Reflection

Why not take a few minutes to read Philippians 2:5–11, noting the striking parallels to this passage in Isaiah? Note the 'servant' who became 'obedient to death', and the equally crucial 'therefore' of the one who went willingly to 'death on a cross' and now is 'exalted to the highest place'. Read, worship and wonder.

Nehemiah: a builder

The words of Nehemiah son of Hacaliah: In the month of Kislev in the twentieth year, while I was in the citadel of Susa, Hanani, one of my brothers, came from Judah with some other men, and I questioned them about the Jewish remnant that survived the exile, and also about Jerusalem. They said to me, 'Those who survived the exile and are back in the province are in great trouble and disgrace. The wall of Jerusalem is broken down, and its gates have been burned with fire.' When I heard these things, I sat down and wept. For some days I mourned and fasted and prayed before the God of heaven. Then I said: 'O Lord, God of heaven, the great and awesome God, who keeps his covenant of love with those who love him and obey his commands, let your ear be attentive and your eyes open to hear the prayer your servant is praying before you day and night for your servants, the people of Israel. I confess the sins we Israelites, including myself and my father's house, have committed against you. We have acted very wickedly towards you. We have not obeyed the commands, decrees and laws you gave your servant Moses. Remember the instruction you gave your servant Moses, saying, "If you are unfaithful, I will scatter you among the nations, but if you return to me and obey my commands, then even if your exiled people are at the farthest

horizon, I will gather them from there and bring them to the place I have chosen as a dwelling for my Name." They are your servants and your people, whom you redeemed by your great strength and your mighty hand. O Lord, let your ear be attentive to the prayer of this your servant and to the prayer of your servants who delight in revering your name. Give your servant success today by granting him favour in the presence of this man.' I was cupbearer to the king.
Nehemiah 1:1–11

To say that Nehemiah is not a name we usually associate with the Christmas story is more than a mild understatement. For many of us, even finding the location of his book is, I suspect, an accomplishment! But I believe he qualifies for a Lifetime Achievement Award for his often overlooked contribution to the the whole motion picture of the kingdom of God and his key part in The Incredible Journey. Really? Wasn't he just a builder, after all is said and done?

Nehemiah lived at a critical period in Israel's history, the fifth century BC. Although now back in their own land, and with a rebuilt temple, all was not well with the Jewish nation. Jerusalem, 'the joy of the whole earth' according to Psalm 48:2, was anything but. Rather, its wall was 'broken down, and its gates... burned with fire'. When the news reached him in 445BC, while he was living some 800 miles away in one of the Persian capitals, Susa, it sent Nehemiah into a tail-spin of fasting, mourning and prayer. Why such angst over a semi-derelict city? One reason was that without a properly constituted and protected city, complete with gates and walls, Jewish identity would be threatened and maybe lost in a hostile world. The last chapter of Nehemiah illustrates the point vividly: it records the previous neglect and abuse of the temple, desecration of the sabbath, mixed marriages and more.

Why did those things matter? The answer lies in a statement of Jesus centuries later, while he was talking to a Samaritan woman: 'Salvation is from the Jews' (John 4:22). This had been part of God's overarching purpose from the day he called Abram to follow him and become the father of a nation through which he intended to bless the world (Genesis 12:1–3). That divine plan, the outworking of which had been underway for centuries, was once again threatened in Nehemiah's time. God's intention was to come to this world personally in Jesus Christ, and through the vehicle of the Jewish people. If that nation became intermingled with other nations and lost, then the bottom line may be starkly expressed: 'No Jews, no Jesus'. 'No Jesus' would mean an aborted rescue mission to the human race.

I'm not suggesting, of course, that Nehemiah had all this figured out in detail. Like the prophets, as the apostle Peter expressed it, he too was 'trying to find out the time and circumstances' concerning the 'sufferings and glories' of Christ (see 1 Peter 1:11–12). But he persisted by serving his own contemporary situation and future generations too.

The first six chapters of the book are stirring stuff. In chapter 1, we meet Nehemiah the worshipper, enjoying intimacy with God—the necessary foundation for any usefulness in God's kingdom. Providentially, as 'cupbearer to the king', he was in an ideal position to influence royal policy. In turn, that influence rewarded him with a governorship in Judah and the role of workman, as the next two chapters illustrate. Faith, courage, vision, tenacity, teamwork and sacrifice are all involved in any great scheme for God. Nehemiah was the type of leader who led from the front. Others recognised his leadership and joined in the great building project. Chapters 4—6 introduce Nehemiah the warrior. God's work is always opposed. Sometimes, it is threatened by outside forces such as Sanballat and his henchmen (Nehemiah 4:7). At other times, there are problems within the camp, as inconsistencies surface within the believing community and abuses have to be dealt with, as in Nehemiah 5. Finally, in the midst of everything else, a leader may often come under sustained scrutiny and personal attack, as chapter 6 makes painfully ,clear.

Are you involved in some work for God? Is it tough? Are you discouraged or tempted to give up? The truth is that many of us often do not see how our small part fits into the 'big picture' of God's ways, but that should not deter us from faithfully doing what is before us day by day. Local churches and projects for the Lord 'grow and build themselves up in love, as each part does its work' (see Ephesians 4:16).

So then, Nehemiah was 'only a builder', yet he passed a lasting legacy on to future generations—Jerusalem, the city of God. To that city, one day, another builder came.[11] Like Nehemiah, he too wept for it (Luke 19:41). Then he did what no one else could do: he suffered 'outside the city gate to make... people holy' and set them on a journey to a 'city that is to come' (Hebrews 13:12, 14). It's called 'the new Jerusalem' (Revelation 21:2). It is Christ's eternal legacy to his people.

Reflection

I am only one,
But still I am one.
I cannot do everything,
But still I can do something;
And because I cannot do everything,
I will not refuse to do the something that I can do.
EDWARD EVERETT HALE (1822–1909)

NOTES

1   John Bright, *The Authority of the Old Testament* (SCM, 1967), pp. 207–208.

2   See Genesis 12:10–20; 16:1–16; 20:1–18; 21:8–21.

3   Genesis 12:7; 13:16; 15:5; 17:8; 1 Kings 2:33; Nehemiah 9:2; Isaiah 6:13; Malachi 2:15.

4   See also verses 16 and 19.

5   See Genesis 46:31–34; Exodus 1:9.

6   M.L. King, *Strength to Love* (Collins, 1963), p. 34.

7   See Genesis 1:1; 12:7; 2 Kings 25; 2 Chronicles 36:21–23.

8   See Matthew 2:6; 5:5; 27:45–46; 28:18–20.

9   Barry Webb, *The Message of Isaiah* (IVP, 1996), p. 212.

10 Alec Motyer, *The Prophecy of Isaiah* (IVP, 1993), p. 442.

11 The Greek *techton*, found in Mark 6:3, is the word used rather dismissively by his 'home crowd' to describe Jesus Christ's daily occupation. From it, in English, we derive words such as 'technical' and 'architect'. It is often translated 'carpenter', but 'builder' is just as acceptable.

22–28 December

ARRIVING ON TIME

It dawned on me for the first time, really. It had dawned on me before, but it really sank in: the Christmas story. The idea that God, if there is a force of Love and Logic in the universe, that it would seek to explain itself is amazing enough. That it would seek to explain itself and describe itself by becoming a child born in straw poverty… a child… I just thought: 'Wow!' Just the poetry… Unknowable love, unknowable power, describes itself as the most vulnerable. There it was. I was sitting there, and it's not that it hadn't struck me before, but tears came down my face, and I saw the genius of this, utter genius of picking a particular point in time, and deciding to turn on this… It's actually logical. It's pure logic. Essence has to manifest itself. It's inevitable. Love has to become an action or something concrete. It would have had to happen. There must be an incarnation. Love must be made flesh.

BONO[1]

Incarnation: impossible!

Then Solomon stood before the altar of the Lord in front of the whole assembly of Israel and spread out his hands. Now he had made a bronze platform, five cubits long, five cubits wide and three cubits high, and had placed it in the centre of the outer court. He stood on the platform and then knelt down before the whole assembly of Israel and spread out his hands towards heaven. He said: 'O Lord, God of Israel, there is no God like you in heaven or on earth—you who keep your covenant of love with your servants who continue wholeheartedly in your way. You have kept your promise to your servant David my father; with your mouth you have promised and with your hand you have fulfilled it—as it is today. Now Lord, God of Israel, keep for your servant David my father the promises you made to him when you said, "You shall never fail to have a man to sit before me on the throne of Israel, if only your sons are careful in all they do to walk before me according to my law, as you have done." And now, O Lord, God of Israel, let your word that you promised your servant David come true. But will God really dwell on earth with men? The heavens, even the highest heavens, cannot contain you. How much less this temple that I have built! Yet give attention to your servant's prayer and his plea for mercy, O Lord my God. Hear the cry and the prayer that your servant is praying in your presence. May your eyes be open towards this temple day and night, this place of which you said you would put your Name there. May you hear the prayer your servant prays towards this place. Hear the supplications of your servant and of your people Israel when they pray towards this place. Hear from heaven, your dwelling-place; and when you hear, forgive.'

2 Chronicles 6:12–21

'But will God really dwell on earth with men?' It's a mind-boggling question when you begin to think about it. It was framed nearly 3000 years ago by one famous for his wisdom, King Solomon, and articulated at the dedication of his magnificent temple. A moment's reflection immediately reminds us that the ancient sage's enquiry has a most contemporary ring and relevance in a world being torn apart by war, facing global economic meltdown and threatened by ecological disaster. Is there anyone up there and out there in that vast cosmos that cares, or are we all alone? Over the next few days we will consider a number of answers to Solomon's question. Today, 'Impossible!' is the first response to consider.

In Great Britain today, there is a rising tide of what is called the 'new atheism'. At one level, of course, the term is misleading. There is nothing new about unbelief. Check out Genesis 3 and our meditations on that chapter earlier in our journey. However, a number of writers and thinkers have grabbed a great deal of media attention and, some of them, huge book sales, through their dogmatic insistence that our universe is the product of blind evolutionary changes. Enough time, chance and impersonal forces have given birth to everything we know and observe.

A little while ago, at Oxford's Museum of Natural History, I attended a debate with the evocative title 'Has science buried God?' Professor Dawkins, as suave and articulate as ever, immediately launched his opening salvos along the lines that the world is beautiful and amazing and, given enough scientific enquiry, eventually we should be able to understand most of what seems mysterious in the universe without recourse to what he termed 'magic'—in other words, a God figure. Stirring stuff! Of course, he did not have the debate all his own way. Professor John Lennox, an Oxford mathematician, multi-linguist and deeply committed orthodox Christian, gave Professor Dawkins more than a run for his money. The implications of Dawkins' atheism emerged at various points during the evening. When questions of justice were raised, he asserted that justice is a mere human construct. Likewise, morality, he believes, is something that societies have made up, as they have developed, so as to get along with each other for mutual benefit. Inevitably at death, therefore, we merely go out like a light—our passing, so far as the universe is concerned, being no more significant than that of a slug.

A friend of mine, as an academic social scientist, has recently been deeply involved in the aftermath of the death of 'Baby Peter', a 17-month-old boy who died after sustaining over 50 injuries during an eight-month period, inflicted by his own mother, her boyfriend and the boyfriend's brother. Public outrage and questions in Parliament only begin to express what any decent-minded person feels—deep revulsion and anger. But why do we think barbarity is so wrong? From where did our sense of right and moral outrage arise in a world where 'dog eats dog'? Will there ever be justice for countless millions of others who likewise have suffered unconscionable wickedness at the hands of countless purveyors of evil? Or is the desire for justice merely a human illusion, a coping mechanism in the face of the absurdity we call life? I realise, of course, that some of my atheist and humanist friends have their counter-arguments and reasons for urging upon us a moral framework in what is, to them, ultimately an absurd universe. Personally, I find none of their reasons convincing or motivating as to why anyone, myself included, should be good.

In contrast, Solomon believed in a God whom the highest heavens could not contain. Nevertheless, he knew God to be utterly reliable, keeping his covenant promises to Israel and hearing and answering prayer, especially for forgiveness. Clearly, therefore, this Lord is already deeply involved in his world. But literally to dwell on earth with us would mean that he would be 'Immanuel—God with us'. That would be impossible, wouldn't it? If not, it would change the way I look at absolutely everything. Our personal response reveals what we really believe about life, its mysteries and its purpose (or utter meaninglessness).

Reflection

The 18th-century hymn writer and friend of John Newton, William Cowper, often struggled with depression and doubt. After one particularly harrowing period of dark despair, he realised that the Lord had been there all along, watching over him. He wrote one of his best-known hymns, 'God moves in a mysterious way' (1774), during that period:

God moves in a mysterious way
His wonders to perform;
He plants His footsteps in the sea
And rides upon the storm.

Judge not the Lord by feeble sense,
But trust Him for His grace;
Behind a frowning providence
He hides a smiling face.

Blind unbelief is sure to err
And scan His work in vain;
God is His own interpreter,
And He will make it plain.

23 December

Incarnation: improbable!

For the director of music. Of the Sons of Korah. According to alamoth. A song.

God is our refuge and strength, an ever-present help in trouble. Therefore we will not fear, though the earth give way and the mountains fall into the heart of the sea, though its waters roar and foam and the mountains quake with their surging. There is a river whose streams make glad the city of God, the holy place where the Most High dwells. God is within her, she will not fall; God will help her at break of day. Nations are in uproar, kingdoms fall; he lifts his voice, the earth melts. The Lord Almighty is with us; the God of Jacob is our fortress. Come and see the works of the Lord, the desolations he has brought on the earth. He makes wars cease to the ends of the earth; he breaks the bow and shatters the spear, he burns the shields with fire. 'Be still, and know that I am God; I will be exalted among the nations, I will be exalted in the earth.' The Lord Almighty is with us; the God of Jacob is our fortress. *Selah*

Psalm 46

Professor Dawkins, in his opening remarks at the debate I mentioned in yesterday's reading, stated rather startlingly, but only in passing, that he felt a case could be made out for the kind of God that Deism describes. The universe does look as if it has been designed—but if so, by whom? In essence, Deism suggests that some great unknown God originally wound up the universe, rather like a clock, and has now left it to run on the laws that physics, chemistry and biology describe. At a popular level, such belief may be expressed, in the words of the title song from the film *Alfie*, as 'something much more, something even unbelievers can believe in'. In terms of the *Star Wars* films, it may be 'the Force' with us in some hard-to-define way. But, of course, there is no room in Deism for personal encounter or relationship with such a God. If he/she/it does exist, given the immensity of the universe of which we are a tiny part, this planet is far too small and insignificant to be bothered about.

Now that is quite a challenge! Given the approximate size of the universe, with its stars and planetary systems, images of which are beamed regularly back to us from the Hubble telescope (feel free to re-read the statistics I mentioned in our reading on 2 December), if there is 'somebody up there', why should that somebody bother about 'us down here'? The brilliant British philosopher Bertrand Russell asked: 'Is man what he seems to the astronomer, a tiny lump of impure carbon and water crawling impotently on a small and unimportant planet? Or is he what he appears to Hamlet? Is he perhaps both at once?'[2] Would the answers to those questions (if we could find them) bring God any nearer? Whatever God may be, surely such a deity would be far too preoccupied with this vast cosmos to be bothered about an insignificant bit of cosmic dust with its near seven billion human inhabitants. Do all our hopes and fears, successes and failures, good and bad choices, living and dying, amount to nothing at all before an indifferent universe/God? In other words, in the grand scheme of things, should we simply conclude that not one of us really matters?

The writer of Psalm 46 has an altogether different answer to the human predicament. He presents a God who is a refuge and hiding place for us when the world seems out of control. Yet this is far from escapism. The Lord Almighty imparts strength to face the world as it is, a place where nations are in uproar and kingdoms totter and fall. He is the God who, according to John Goldingay's translation, 'always offers himself as a help in times of trouble.' Accordingly, 'God does not guarantee that trouble will not come to those who trust in him. But he does guarantee that, when trouble comes, he will be the rock that saves us, the citadel that protects us, the tower that frustrates our enemies.'[3] Therefore, his people need not give way to fear. Ultimately, according to the psalmist, God intends to bring an end to war and evil of every kind. Thereby, the psalm anticipates the prophecy of Isaiah, who foresaw the day when 'every warrior's boot used in battle' would be 'destined for burning' (Isaiah 9:5). And how would that be accomplished? Through a child:

For to us a child is born,
to us a son is given,
and the government will be on his shoulders.
And he will be called
Wonderful Counsellor, Mighty God,
Everlasting Father, Prince of Peace.

Of the increase of his government and peace
there will be no end.
He will reign on David's throne
and over his kingdom,
establishing and upholding it
with justice and righteousness
from that time on and forever.
The zeal of the Lord Almighty
will accomplish this. (Isaiah 9:6–7)

Christmas is often one of the busiest periods of the year, but Psalm 46 invites us to 'be still and know that I am God', to consider the child who has come to change everything. The psalm concludes with the word 'Selah', which translates as something like, 'Pause, and think of that!'[4]

Reflection

They all were looking for a king
To slay their foes and lift them high:
Thou cam'st, a little baby thing
That made a woman cry.
GEORGE MACDONALD (1883)

'Selah' indeed!

24 December

Incarnation: inevitable!

Dear friends, let us love one another, for love comes from God. Everyone who loves has been born of God and knows God. Whoever does not love does not know God, because God is love. This is how God showed his love among us: he sent his one and only Son into the world that we might live through him. This is love: not that we loved God, but that he loved us and sent his Son as an atoning sacrifice for our sins. Dear friends, since God so loved us, we also ought to love one another. No-one has ever seen God; but if we love one another, God lives in us and his love is made complete in us. We know that we live in him and he in us, because he has given us of his Spirit. And we have seen and testify that the Father has sent his Son to be the Saviour of the world. If anyone acknowledges that Jesus is the Son of God, God lives in him and he in God. And so we know and rely on the love God has for us. God is love. Whoever lives in love lives in God, and God in him. In this way, love is made complete among us so that we will have confidence on the day of judgment, because in this world we are like him. There is no fear in love. But perfect love drives out fear, because fear has to do with punishment. The one who fears is not made perfect in love. We love because he first loved us. If anyone says, 'I love God,' yet hates his brother, he is a liar. For anyone who does not love his brother, whom he has seen, cannot love God, whom he has not seen. And he has given us this command: Whoever loves God must also love his brother.

1 John 4:7–21

The parish church that I attended as a child and where I sang in the choir had a biblical text emblazoned across the wall behind the altar: 'God is love'. Whatever else may be predicated of him, this is the bottom line: God's essence is love. Yet what an abused word 'love' is, so easily misunderstood and often used merely as a synonym for sex. Nevertheless, there is something almost intuitive in each of us that can recognise 'real love' when we see it. It is the very opposite of the greedy, self-promoting, 'me first' self-interest that is nothing other than obnoxious selfishness. If God is love, then love must be expressed not only towards and in himself but outwards to others. Richard Harries, when he was Bishop of Oxford, wrote movingly about a moment of insight that led to his belief in the incarnation:

Sitting in a gaunt German barrack block in 1957 I was struck by the thesis of Aldous Huxley's Perennial Philosophy that at the heart of every religion is the paradox that we find ourselves by losing ourselves; that we discover our true self by giving ourselves away. In one of those life-changing moments of insight two thoughts quickly followed and merged into one conviction. If this paradox is at the heart of every religion, then this must be the best clue we have as to the nature of ultimate reality. And if God himself is like this, then what

more sublime expression of giving oneself away could there be than
the incarnation, the immortal becoming as mortal and vulnerable as
any other human person? The train of thought was not the logic of
philosophy but of love. If God is a God of love how can we not believe
in the incarnation?[5]

In today's reading, three profound phrases capture that
thought of the love of God in incarnational love:

- This is how God showed his love among us: he sent
  his one and only Son into the world that we might live
  through him (v. 9).
- This is love: not that we loved God, but that he loved us
  and sent his Son as an atoning sacrifice for our sins (v. 10).
- And we have seen and testify that the Father has sent his
  Son to be the Saviour of the world (v. 14).

Three questions suggest themselves. Whom did God send?
Why? What did it achieve?

Whom did God send? 'His one and only Son.' This is the
apostle John's way of expressing the uniqueness of Jesus.
When he speaks of believers, John calls us 'children of
God', because we are adopted into God's family. So there
is a 'start time' to our relationship with God. But the Son
whom God sent never had a 'start time' to his relationship
with his Father. As a preacher once memorably put it, 'Jesus
is older than his mother and as old as his Father!' God sent
us in Jesus, we might say, 'his very heart'—the Son whom he
always loved. And the reason was that 'we might live through
him'—that is, have eternal life.

So why did God send Jesus? 'As an atoning sacrifice for our sins.' Over 50 years ago, Harry Belafonte, a well-known American singer, recorded a No 1 hit, a delightful Christmas song called 'Mary's boy child'. Its words assured us that we may live for ever more because of Christmas Day. Not quite! For sure, we can't live for ever more without Christmas Day, but something more was needed. The barrier of our sin needed to be addressed and dealt with too. So, to his cradle Christ added a cross.

What did Christ's coming and cross achieve? 'The Father has sent his Son to be the Saviour of the world.' In the film *Superman Returns*, Superman asks Lois Lane why she has written an article against him. She replies, 'I moved on. So did the rest of us. That's why I wrote it. The world doesn't need a saviour. And neither do I.' He responds, 'Listen…' She says, 'I don't hear anything.' He replies movingly, 'I do. I hear everything. You wrote that the world doesn't need a saviour, but every day I hear people crying for one.' Does God hear that cry of humanity?

The story of the exodus occurred because the Lord said, 'I have indeed seen the misery of my people… I have heard them crying… So I have come down to rescue them' (Exodus 3:7–8).[6] In Jesus Christ a new exodus is underway. God has come down to rescue us and take us to a promised land that will never end. Jesus Christ is not a comic book hero, a fictional Superman. He is something much, much more—a real space–time Saviour.

Reflection

Let earth and heaven combine,
Angels and men agree,
To praise in songs divine
The incarnate Deity;
Our God contracted to a span,
Incomprehensibly made Man.

CHARLES WESLEY (1744)

25 December

Saviour's Day

In the beginning was the Word, and the Word was with God, and the Word was God. He was with God in the beginning. Through him all things were made; without him nothing was made that has been made. In him was life, and that life was the light of men. The light shines in the darkness, but the darkness has not understood it. There came a man who was sent from God; his name was John. He came as a witness to testify concerning that light, so that through him all men might believe. He himself was not the light; he came only as a witness to the light. The true light that gives light to every man was coming into the world. He was in the world, and though the world was made through him, the world did not recognise him. He came to that which was his own, but his own did not receive him. Yet to all who received him, to those who believed in his name, he gave the right to become children of God—children born not of natural descent, nor of human decision or a husband's will, but born of God. The Word became flesh and made his dwelling among us. We have seen his glory, the glory of the One and Only, who came from the Father, full of grace and truth. John testifies concerning him. He cries out, saying, 'This was he of whom I said, "He who comes after me has surpassed me because he was before me."' From the fullness of his grace we have

all received one blessing after another. For the law was given
through Moses; grace and truth came through Jesus Christ.
No-one has ever seen God, but God the One and Only, who
is at the Father's side, has made him known.
John 1:1–18

A six-year-old girl seemed unusually quiet and focused as,
bent over her drawing, she worked tirelessly away in art
class. Eventually, her teacher enquired about her work. 'I'm
drawing a picture of God!' she insisted. 'But no one knows
what God looks like,' the teacher gently responded. 'They
will in a minute!' came the confident reply. We may smile at
the child's precocity, yet also pause to note that both teacher
and pupil had a point.

'No one has ever seen God,' John reminds us. Images of
God were strictly forbidden in Judaism. There were to be no
pictures of God. How could there be, since he is invisible—
'pure Spirit', we might say? And yet, John adds, Jesus Christ
has 'made him known'. The word underlying that translation (from the Greek) is 'exegeted'. If preachers do their
homework on a Bible passage, making its meaning clear,
they are good 'exegetes': they bring out what is there. Well,
Jesus Christ is the exegete par excellence: he has explained,
guided, narrated, brought out, revealed and detailed God.
In that sense, he is the authorised and authentic picture of
God. What is God like? He is just like Jesus: How else could
we explain his astonishing claim, 'Anyone who has seen me
has seen the Father' (John 14:9)? How can that be? It all
turns on what has been described as the most remarkable
and mysterious verse in the Bible:

The Word became flesh and made his dwelling among us. We have seen his glory, the glory of the One and Only, who came from the Father, full of grace and truth (John 1:14).

This verse makes a number of monumental assertions:

- The deity of Jesus: the Word
- The humanity of Jesus: flesh
- The humility of Jesus: among us
- The majesty of Jesus: the One and Only
- The mercy of Jesus: full of grace and truth

Allow me briefly to 'exegete' some of the foregoing.

Theologians have endlessly debated the background of the phrase 'the Word'. Is it to be understood from its use in Greek philosophy or Old Testament thought? What is clear is that God has eternally been able to express himself, and that creative expression is not merely a thought but a person: 'In the beginning was the Word, and the Word was with God, and the Word was God' (v. 1). Here the Word's eternity, closest proximity to the Father and own essential deity are all asserted. There never was a time when the Word was not, and that Word became 'flesh', a real human being. Many people baulk at the truth claims of Christianity, involving miracles, Jesus as the way to God, his resurrection and so on. But here is the greatest miracle of all—God becoming man. As Queen Lucy puts it in C.S. Lewis's book *The Last Battle*, 'a Stable once held something inside it that was bigger than our whole world'.[7] If that is true, then turning water into wine, healing the sick, calming storms and raising the dead are the very things we would expect of an incarnate God.

It would be easy to overlook the depth of humility contained in the phrase 'made his dwelling among us'. Who has not enjoyed hearing the stories of some of life's great entrepreneurs and others who have risen via rags to riches? But in Jesus we see the divine paradox. It is a 'riches to rags' story being played out. He who was 'at the Father's side' as 'the true light' of God, who enjoyed the company of angels and spirits purer than we can conceive, stepped into our darkness, stooping to join the human race. In coming to save the world, Jesus changed addresses and became one of us. Likewise, since then, the incarnation principle—coming to where people are—has been at the heart of all true Christian mission to the world. So missionaries like J. Hudson Taylor, who spent over 50 years in China, have followed Christ's example, changing locations, learning a foreign language, adopting local customs and clothing, in order to bring good news to the world.

Let us rejoice this Christmas Day that God's eternal Son, his 'One and Only... full of grace and truth', has brought light for our darkness and hope for our despair. Happy Christmas!

Reflection

'The omnipotent, in one instant, made himself breakable. He who had been spirit became pierceable. He who was larger than the universe became an embryo. And he who sustains the world with a word chose to be dependent upon the nourishment of a young girl. God as a fetus. Holiness sleeping in a womb. The creator of life being created. God was given eyebrows, elbows, two kidneys, and a spleen. He stretched against the walls and floated in the amniotic fluids of his mother.'

MAX LUCADO[8]

See, amid the winter's snow,
Born for us on earth below,
See, the Lamb of God appears,
Promised from eternal years.

Lo, within a manger lies
He who built the starry skies,
He who, throned in height sublime,
Sits amid the cherubim.

Hail, that ever-blessèd morn!
Hail, redemption's happy dawn!
Sing through all Jerusalem:
Christ is born in Bethlehem!
EDWARD CASWALL (1814–78)

26 December

Mother's Day

In the sixth month, God sent the angel Gabriel to Nazareth, a town in Galilee, to a virgin pledged to be married to a man named Joseph, a descendant of David. The virgin's name was Mary. The angel went to her and said, 'Greetings, you who are highly favoured! The Lord is with you.' Mary was greatly troubled at his words and wondered what kind of greeting this might be. But the angel said to her, 'Do not be afraid, Mary, you have found favour with God. You will be with child and give birth to a son, and you are to give him the name Jesus. He will be great and will be called the Son of the Most High. The Lord God will give him the throne of his father David, and he will reign over the house of Jacob for ever; his kingdom will never end.' 'How will this be,' Mary asked the angel, 'since I am a virgin?' The angel answered, 'The Holy Spirit will come upon you, and the power of the Most High will overshadow you. So the holy one to be born will be called the Son of God. Even Elizabeth your relative is going to have a child in her old age, and she who was said to be barren is in her sixth month. For nothing is impossible with God.' 'I am the Lord's servant,' Mary answered. 'May it be to me as you have said.' Then the angel left her.

Luke 1:26–38

There are two equal and opposite errors into which we can fall about the Virgin Mary. One is to disbelieve that she was a virgin mother. The other is to believe and to feel an excessive and unhealthy interest in her. She herself, I suspect, would be equally displeased by both errors.[9] Although today is not, of course, 'St Mary's Day' (it is, in fact, officially St Stephen's Day), is there a fitting way to celebrate this particular mother's 'Day'?

First, it is appropriate to acknowledge this young woman's calling. Gabriel greets her as 'highly favoured'. How highly? The answer lies in the nature of her calling. It was she who was the chosen vessel for what every pious believer in Israel longed for—the coming of the Messiah. At last, after centuries of promise, a new king would be born whose 'kingdom will never end', reigning 'over the house of Jacob for ever', and his name would be 'Jesus'. However, there was a problem. Although pledged to be married, Mary lived in a society that practised 'love, marriage and sex' in that order. So 'How will this be?' she rightly asks. Enter what is termed 'the virgin birth' or, as some prefer, 'the virgin conception'.

At this juncture, all sorts of opinions and reactions begin to emerge. Some have suggested that Luke and Matthew misunderstood (perhaps deliberately) the meaning of the Hebrew word used in Isaiah 7:14, which prophesied that a 'virgin' would conceive a child. They say that the word simply meant 'a young woman', not 'a virgin girl'. Others believe that the story of the virgin conception is just a myth—a way of talking up the significance of some leader or heroine by assigning them a special start in life, when everyone knows full well that it never actually happened that way. Sometimes, in support of this belief, parallels are produced from ancient legends and other cultures and religions. For many, the virgin birth is dismissed as a straightforward biological impossibility (as if that realisation had never occurred to the physician Luke, of all people, or anybody else in the early Church).[10] Of course it is humanly impossible—but 'nothing is impossible with God' is the angel's riposte. Graham Leonard, when Bishop of London, expressed it this way:

When a man begets and a woman conceives a child a new person is created, a person who has not previously existed. The Creeds were hammered out to affirm in unmistakable and unequivocal terms that by the conception and birth of Jesus of Nazareth no new person was created. What happened was that the second person of the Trinity entered into a new relationship with the world, which he had created, and united a human body and a human nature to himself. In other words, the man who grew up in Palestine, exercised a public ministry, and then suffered a criminal's death was no other than God himself... That being so, it was wholly congruous for the manner of his conception to differ from that of a new person.[11]

Mary's courage should be noted. Her cousin Elizabeth could rejoice that she had conceived in her old age, thus ending the 'disgrace' (Luke 1:25) that her culture imposed on anyone who was childless. In contrast, for Mary to conceive a child out of wedlock was a 'public disgrace' (Matthew 1:19). In other words, what God was asking of her was totally counter-cultural, leaving her vulnerable to criticism and misunderstanding. Her response, 'May it be to me as you have said', is the same kind of willingness that says, 'Here am I. Send me!' (Isaiah 6:8) Are we that willing and available to God?

Eventually, Mary visited her cousin Elizabeth and they compared notes—as pregnant women often rightly do. Echoing the song of Hannah, another surprised mother from centuries before (1 Samuel 2:1–10), Luke records Mary's magnificent Magnificat (see 'Reflection' below). In it, Mary expresses her gratitude to God, her Saviour, for choosing her, 'lowly as she is' (v. 48, REB). Then follows a form of speech common in the Old Testament: God's future acts are expressed in the past tense as if they had already happened, so sure is the speaker that they will come to pass. Mary declares the kind of moral, religious, social and economic revolution that the coming of God's kingdom in Christ will mean: the proud resisted, (evil) rulers overthrown and the hungry satisfied. All this will take place because God made promises to Abraham and his 'seed'[12] centuries before.

Years ago, a retired missionary to China shared with me the way the old Chinese language used pictures to illustrate concepts. A man standing next to a mouth represented 'faithfulness'. In other words, a person who stands by their words is reliable. So is God! When we rely and act on the Lord's promises, that is called 'faith', since we are relying on his faithfulness. Such faith will not produce a virgin birth, but, like Mary, and encouraged by our own experience of God, we discover in Christ that 'the Mighty One has done great things' for us and will continue to do so. Mary believed that. Shouldn't we?

Reflection

My soul glorifies the Lord
and my spirit rejoices in God my Saviour,
for he has been mindful
of the humble state of his servant.
From now on all generations will call me blessed,
for the Mighty One has done great things for me—
holy is his name.
His mercy extends to those who fear him,
from generation to generation.
He has performed mighty deeds with his arm;
he has scattered those who are proud in their inmost thoughts.
He has brought down rulers from their thrones
but has lifted up the humble.
He has filled the hungry with good things
but has sent the rich away empty.
He has helped his servant Israel,
remembering to be merciful
to Abraham and his descendants for ever,
even as he said to our fathers.

LUKE 1:46–55

27 December

Father's Day

This is how the birth of Jesus Christ came about: his mother Mary was pledged to be married to Joseph, but before they came together, she was found to be with child through the Holy Spirit. Because Joseph her husband was a righteous man and did not want to expose her to public disgrace, he had in mind to divorce her quietly. But after he had considered this, an angel of the Lord appeared to him in a dream and said, 'Joseph son of David, do not be afraid to take Mary home as your wife, because what is conceived in her is from the Holy Spirit. She will give birth to a son, and you are to give him the name Jesus, because he will save his people from their sins.' All this took place to fulfil what the Lord had said through the prophet: 'The virgin will be with child and will give birth to a son, and they will call him Immanuel—which means, God with us.' When Joseph woke up, he did what the angel of the Lord had commanded him and took Mary home as his wife. But he had no union with her until she gave birth to a son. And he gave him the name Jesus.

Matthew 1:18–25

Being the son (as was supposed) of Joseph.
Luke 3:23 (ESV)

The pain suffered by the victims of personal betrayal can be immense, and when the facts are in the public domain, the sufferer's wretchedness can be indescribable. Given the culture of his day, the confines of a small town and his daily job as a carpenter, Joseph would have found nowhere to hide his feelings or himself when the 'balloon went up' with the news of his fiancée's pregnancy. Shock, anger, confusion and revulsion are all reactions that easily spring to mind. It's the stuff of literature, film and a thousand TV dramas: a soldier returns from his tour of duty in a war zone, or a prisoner is released after a period inside, only to discover that his partner is pregnant by someone else. A wife wonders whether her husband's recent overseas business trip is related to the STD she has suddenly contracted. How do you get through when your personal world is pulled apart or smashed into a thousand pieces by someone you loved and trusted—a spouse, a parent, a child or a close friend?

If we are 'self-righteous', we quickly become judge, jury and executioner of those who have offended and hurt us and ours. Joseph was not 'self righteous' but 'righteous'—a man of faith, a good man. So he refused to sample the poisonous delicacy called revenge, and determined to do the right thing as he saw it, deciding 'to divorce quietly' his beloved Mary. As THE MESSAGE translates it, he took some time 'to figure a way out'. However much his heart was breaking, such a course of action was infinitely preferable to a knee-jerk reaction that might later be regretted, no matter how much justifiable anger he may have felt.

In refusing to 'rush in where angels fear to tread', Joseph left space for God to work. In his case, it was during a dream that an angel of the Lord delivered a message that confirmed Mary's story, changed his mind and told him about a child who would change the world. How can you possibly corroborate a dream like that? Perhaps the answer came during a service he was attending at his local synagogue. Maybe the ancient prophecy of a 'virgin being with child' was read, and wonderfully confirmed his nocturnal visitor's words. Likewise, it is still marvellous when God speaks to us as believers gather for worship and teaching. Who knows how it happened for Joseph? But it is always right to check out our hopes and dreams against scripture. It would save many individuals and churches from some real nightmares.

It was a bold step of obedience for Joseph to do what had been 'commanded him'. His obedience would entail his being a stepdad for years to come. Who knows what gossip and innuendo he, Mary and their family would have had to endure? Some find an echo of that gossip when, years later in his home town, Jesus is scathingly referred to as 'the carpenter's son' (Matthew 13:55)—or again, in another confrontation, when his opponents remind Jesus that they are 'not illegitimate children' (John 8:41).

Are you in some form of 'step' relationship? Recently, I was chatting to a young man who is a stepson. 'Charlie is not my real dad,' he was protesting—but Charlie had carried out all the functions of a 'real dad', biology apart, for that yet-to-be-grateful teenager. So I reminded him about someone whose 'real dad' happened to run the universe but whose 'supposed dad' was Joseph. Through that supposed dad, Jesus was cared for and protected (remember the flight into Egypt: Matthew 2:14), learned to speak and to read God's word, was taught a trade and was trained in a thousand other ways for life. Although destined to be the Saviour of the world, Jesus was obedient to his human parents (Luke 2:51). Can you imagine that Jesus was ever rude to his stepdad? Can you? Neither can I.

One final thing. Although he was commanded to marry Mary, Joseph did not simply 'do the decent thing' for a young, vulnerable, pregnant woman in need of a husband. He was engaged to a woman he loved and thought he had lost. That's one of the reasons he attempted to avoid exposing her to public disgrace and was heading for a quiet divorce. So his obedience did not go against the grain of what he really wanted. Love makes burdens light. It's great when the Lord tells you to do what you really wanted to do anyway!

Reflection

'The better part of valour is discretion,' Shakespeare reminds us.[13] *Joseph exercised such discretion, as we might say, 'in spades'. Are there areas where we need to do likewise, especially in our families and close relationships?*

28 December

Friends' Day

After Jesus was born in Bethlehem in Judea, during the time of King Herod, Magi from the east came to Jerusalem and asked, 'Where is the one who has been born king of the Jews? We saw his star in the east and have come to worship him.' When King Herod heard this he was disturbed, and all Jerusalem with him. When he had called together all the people's chief priests and teachers of the law, he asked them where the Christ was to be born. 'In Bethlehem in Judea,' they replied, 'for this is what the prophet has written: "But you, Bethlehem, in the land of Judah, are by no means least among the rulers of Judah; for out of you will come a ruler who will be the shepherd of my people Israel."' Then Herod called the Magi secretly and found out from them the exact time the star had appeared. He sent them to Bethlehem and said, 'Go and make a careful search for the child. As soon as you find him, report to me, so that I too may go and worship him.' After they had heard the king, they went on their way, and the star they had seen in the east went ahead of them until it stopped over the place where the child was. When they saw the star, they were overjoyed. On coming to the house, they saw the child with his mother Mary, and they bowed down and worshipped him. Then they opened their treasures and presented him with gifts of gold and of incense and of myrrh. And having been warned in a dream not to go back to Herod, they returned to their country by another route.

Matthew 2:1–12

Patrick Moore, the well-known astronomer and broadcaster, dismissing the idea that astrology is in any way scientific, cuttingly remarked that its only truth is 'There's one born every minute!' The Old Testament both lampoons and prohibits astrology, although the practice was widespread in the first century, even among the Jews.[14] This passage neither sanctions nor condemns it. Rather, the behaviour of the magi is contrasted with that of Herod and the Jewish leaders. We can identify three different kinds of behaviour:

- The apathy of the religious leaders
- The antagonism of Herod
- The adoration of the magi

Bethlehem was a mere six miles from Jerusalem, a couple of hours' journey on foot. Yet it was clearly a journey too far for the scholars and theologians of the day to see 'the king of the Jews'. Clearly they knew their Bibles, quoting chapter and verse from Micah as to the precise location of the Messiah's birth. But when it came to acting upon that knowledge and hurrying down the road to Bethlehem, they were totally indifferent. Apathy can destroy any life! I recall a clever piece of graffito on a university wall: 'Apathy rul'. That's no typo: apathy often can't be bothered to start, much less to finish. It is possible to be highly educated, well connected and religious, just as these leaders were, and yet to miss Jesus Christ when he arrives just down the road and outside the tight social, intellectual, religious or financial box that we term 'reality'.

The reaction of Herod the Great, as he is now known, was altogether different. He was a crafty, wealthy, politically smart operator who had managed to stay in favour with successive emperors in Rome, after being named king of Judea by the Roman senate in 40BC. Is it credible that he would have given orders, as the verses after today's reading record, to kill all the boys in Bethlehem who were aged two and under? Sadly, it is all too possible. Towards the end of his life, in his raging paranoia, he arranged the murders of his wife Mariamne, at least two of his sons and other close associates. The idea that there was a legitimate 'king of the Jews' (which he was not, because he was of Idumean descent) could only fuel his fury. We note that from the beginning of his earthly life, Jesus never lacked enemies, and the growing antagonism to him, recorded in the Gospels, would culminate in his crucifixion. It should be no surprise if his ongoing cause in the world today generates intense opposition at times.

The magi had a very different agenda: 'we have come to worship him' (v. 2). If the magi came from Babylon, where there was a large Jewish community, it is plausible that they had read the Old Testament, containing its promise that 'a star will come out of Jacob' (Numbers 24:17). Regular attempts have been made to match the particular star they saw with various astronomical phenomena, including Halley's Comet and supernovas. The hardest explanation is also the simplest, however: it was a supernatural 'star' that heralded the coming of the one whose hands had created the stars in the first place.

Down the centuries, commentators have attached symbolic significance to each of the gifts presented by the magi. The carol 'We three kings of Orient are' assigns gold to Christ's royalty, frankincense to his deity and myrrh to his sacrificial death and burial. Someone has facetiously remarked that if they had been wise women rather then men, the gifts would have been more practical—nappies, bottles, baby clothes and so on! However, as Jesus would have been nearly two years old by the time the magi arrived, these items may not have been so practical after all. Whatever their symbolic significance, in financial terms they were expensive gifts. Who knows whether their immediate usefulness became apparent in funding their flight down into Egypt?

In conclusion, it is important to note the main reason why these magi are included in Matthew's story. The Old Testament foresaw a day when gifts would be brought to Israel's ideal king and the nations would come to his light.[15] Although he would be born king of the Jews, his coming would be for all people. That is one reason why Jesus is called the Saviour of the world. The wise worshipped him. They still do.

Reflection

I cannot tell how all the lands shall worship,
When, at his bidding, every storm is stilled,
Or who can say how great the jubilation
When every heart with perfect love is filled.

But this I know, the skies will thrill with rapture,
And myriad, myriad human voices sing,
And earth to heaven, and heaven to earth, will answer:
'At last the Saviour, Saviour of the world, is King!'
WILLIAM YOUNG FULLERTON (1929)

NOTES

1 Michka Assayas, *Bono on Bono: Conversations with Michka Assayas* (Hodder & Stoughton, 2005), p. 125.
2 Quoted by Ken Robinson, *The Element* (Penguin, 2009), p. 59.
3 John Goldingay, *Songs from a Strange Land* (IVP, 1978), pp. 96, 103.
4 The Amplified Bible.
5 Richard Harries, 'Moment of insight that led to belief in the incarnation', *The Times* (24 December 1990).
6 See the reading for 17 December.
7 C.S. Lewis, *The Last Battle* (Penguin, 1971, first published 1956), p. 128.
8 Quoted by Sam Storms in his blog, 'Enjoying God Ministries', December 2005, from Max Lucado's *God Came Near* (W Publishing, 2004).
9 I am consciously parodying an astute remark about devils in C.S. Lewis's *The Screwtape Letters* (Geoffrey Bles, 1942), p. 9. Obviously, there is no intended parallel to be drawn between them and the Blessed Virgin Mary!
10 On these and other related issues surrounding Matthew and Luke's claims, Gresham Machen's *The Virgin Birth of Christ* (James Clarke, 1958) is still worth consulting.
11 Graham Leonard, 'The Coherence of the Life of Jesus', *The Times* (13 September 1984).
12 Note the recurrence of 'seed', for which see our reading on 14 December.
13 Falstaff in *Henry IV Part 1*, Act V, scene 4.
14 See Isaiah 47:13–15; Jeremiah 10:2 and also the judicious comments on this passage in D.A. Carson's *Matthew*, The Expositors' Bible Commentary, Vol 8 (Zondervan, 1984), to which I gladly acknowledge my indebtedness in preparing this day's reading.
15 For example, see Psalm 72:10–11; Isaiah 60:3, 6.

29 December–4 January

JOURNEYING ON

The book of Revelation was written 'to encourage saints to press on, despite all opposition, and to win the inheritance… that [they] might enter the city of God, and the vision of the city is the true climax of the book—its goal, not simply its finis.'

GEORGE BEASLEY-MURRAY[1]

29 December

Living Lord

I, John, your brother and companion in the suffering and kingdom and patient endurance that are ours in Jesus, was on the island of Patmos because of the word of God and the testimony of Jesus. On the Lord's Day I was in the Spirit, and I heard behind me a loud voice like a trumpet, which said: 'Write on a scroll what you see and send it to the seven churches: to Ephesus, Smyrna, Pergamum, Thyatira, Sardis, Philadelphia and Laodicea.' I turned round to see the voice that was speaking to me. And when I turned I saw seven golden lampstands, and among the lampstands was someone like a son of man, dressed in a robe reaching down to his feet and with a golden sash round his chest. His head and hair were white like wool, as white as snow, and his eyes were like blazing fire. His feet were like bronze glowing in a furnace, and his voice was like the sound of rushing waters. In his right hand he held seven stars, and out of his mouth came a sharp double-edged sword. His face was like the sun shining in all its brilliance. When I saw him, I fell at his feet as though dead. Then he placed his right hand on me and said: 'Do not be afraid. I am the First and the Last. I am the Living One; I was dead, and behold I am alive for ever and ever! And I hold the keys of death and Hades.'

Revelation 1:9–18

I'd travelled down that road a thousand times. I was just ten minutes or so from home, but there was no moonlight that night, and that part of the A338 had no artificial lighting. It was shortly after 10.30pm and, after a couple of hours of driving, I was looking forward to supper and bed. Presently, in the distance on the tree-lined dual carriageway, I saw a small, dim light that seemed to be moving slowly as I raced towards it at 70 mph. Suddenly, my mental 'lights' came on: it turned out to be, as I later discovered, a slow-moving, very poorly lit moped. Without any feelings of heroism, I swerved to avoid the inevitable collision, lost control of the car and, praying and braking furiously, headed at speed into the trees. It's a well-known accident black spot there on the A338: it has regularly claimed lives, usually because, if you argue with a tree, however big your car, you tend to lose. When there's a whole forest of them, your chance of winning can be measured, I suspect, by comparing it to a major lottery win—a very long shot. To this day, I don't know what it was, humanly speaking, that flipped my car and landed it and me upside down, nestling between two banks of trees with a huge ditch in between. That ditch kept the car's roof and my head on. Except for a few scratches, I walked away unscathed and have lived to write this tale.

What has this to do with Revelation 1? In my case, quite a lot. The nursing staff at my local hospital, checking me out until the early hours of the morning, kept reminding me how lucky I was to be alive. I continued to reiterate my take on the accident: 'I'm a committed Christian, and Jesus assures me that he has "the keys of death and Hades". Until he says so, I'm not going anywhere!' Some of the staff probably put my reaction down to being hit on the head in the accident.

The early Christians who first heard these words certainly needed such assurance. Difficult times were in store for them. If the book of Revelation was composed in the last decade of the first century, as many scholars believe, big troubles were ahead in the form of the Emperor Domitian— 'a cruel monster' according to Pliny the Younger, one of his contemporaries. Persecution was on the way, so Christians in places like ancient Philadelphia would not be the only ones to feel as if they had 'little strength' (Revelation 3:8). All believers would need the assurance that Christ's keeping power in 'the hour of trial that is going to come upon the whole world' (v. 10) would be sufficient. That's why this opening chapter of Revelation is so important. John is given a breathtaking vision of the majesty and power of Jesus Christ. The reason Christ holds the keys of death is that he both died and has now conquered death, and is 'alive for ever and ever'.

We may think of our lives, on The Incredible Journey, like travelling down a long, long motorway, with various exits indicated along the way. For most of the time those inter-sections are coned off and barred to us. One day, however, each of us will approach our designated exit. The turning-off point will be unavoidable and unmistakable. It will be my personal departure from the journey of my life. It is marked 'death'. But when I belong to Jesus Christ, I can be confident that it will only be opened when he, the keeper of the keys of my destiny, removes the cones and guides me on to the slip road that leads into his immediate presence.

A thousand years before the resurrection, David was confident that 'all the days ordained for me were written in your book before one of them came to be' (Psalm 139:16). I don't know about you, but I find that a comforting thought as I hurtle towards a new year with all its hopes and uncertainties. Of course I don't know why Tom in old age, Dick in middle years or Harriet in early life had to die when they did: no one knows the 'why' of each individual's death. But if Jesus, the living Lord, has the keys of death, then I can relax a little: I'm going to die right on time! That's a massive enough reason in a world of immense uncertainty 'not to be afraid'.

Anyone for a drive in my new car?

Reflection

Lord, let it not be said of me, 'He died at 35, but he was not buried till he was 83!' If I am going to die on time, then help me to imitate the heroes of old who 'were still living by faith when they died' (Hebrews 11:13). And while I am here on earth, may I live every day to your glory. Amen

30 December

Messy Church

Ephesus (Sound Street Abbey)
I know that you cannot tolerate wicked men... Yet... you have forsaken your first love.
Revelation 2:2, 4

Smyrna (Crown Close Cathedral)
Be faithful, even to the point of death, and I will give you the crown of life.
Revelation 2:10

Pergamum (Martyr's Memorial Mission)
Antipas, my faithful witness, who was put to death in your city—where Satan lives.
Revelation 2:13

Thyatira (Loose Lane Fellowship)
You are now doing more than you did at first. Nevertheless... you tolerate that woman Jezebel.
Revelation 2:19–20

Sardis (Cemetery Junction Church)
You have a reputation of being alive, but you are dead.
Revelation 3:1

Philadelphia (Main Road Assembly)
I have placed before you an open door that no one can shut.
I know that you have little strength.
Revelation 3:8

Laodicea (Cool Court Chapel)
So, because you are lukewarm—neither hot nor cold—I am
about to spit you out of my mouth.
Revelation 3:16

Messy Church® is a recent initiative being rolled out in an
increasing number of churches around the UK and abroad.
As a movement, it aims to provide 'fresh ideas for building a
Christ-centred community'.[2] I think it's a great title, for (like
me, I suspect) many of us have often found our local church
to be anything but pristine. Yes, 'messy' is a good summary
of many churches I've known, visited, been a member of and
had the privilege of pastoring. Is that a depressing thought? It
is not intended to be—just the opposite, in fact.

Over the years, I have met some good and well-meaning
Christians who have regularly harped on about our need to be
'a New Testament church' and to 'get back to it' via renewal,
repentance, reformation, revival or restoration (choose which
'R' is your preferred route). At a number of levels, I know what
they mean and share their aspirations for 'a radiant church,
without stain or wrinkle or any other blemish' (Ephesians
5:27). However, as the German theologian Dietrich Bonhoeffer
expressed it, we must learn to love the real church, not just
the ideal church. It is the 'real church' we are introduced to
in these two chapters of Revelation—churches battling it out

at the end of the tough first century. Through them, Jesus still addresses 21st-century Christians and churches who, likewise, are in need of hope and encouragement, or rebuke and challenge as well.

These seven churches of ancient Asia Minor were very similar in one respect: they all needed to hear the word of God from Jesus. However, they were very different in terms of what they needed to hear and how they needed to respond. Ephesus, for instance, was very much 'Sound Street Abbey'—thoroughly orthodox. It could not 'tolerate wicked men', yet, sadly, like a partner in a marriage lacking passion and merely going through the motions, it had forsaken its first love for Jesus Christ. Smyrna, 'Crown Close Cathedral', was prepared to be faithful 'even to the point of death' and was promised a 'crown of life'. There was no way the Smyrnans were going to be unfaithful to Christ in dark days. Pergamum was already 'Martyr's Memorial Mission'. It had a great history because of Antipas, its witness/martyr. However, since past performance is no guarantee of future growth, as various financial institutions warn us, its future well-being was being threatened by false teaching. Then, down the road, there was 'Loose Lane Fellowship', Thyatira. This was a really active church but mistakenly thought that its industry would balance out the immorality tolerated within itself. Ignoring the symptoms of a cancer is no way to ensure its cure.

Next, there was 'Cemetery Junction Church', Sardis. Clearly, this church had a great PR machine and regularly let everyone know just how 'alive' it was. Strangely, Jesus did not believe its publicity and judged it to be both fast asleep and 'dead'. In stark contrast, however, there was 'Main Road Assembly',

Philadelphia. This church really did have great opportunities. Wherever it turned, 'open doors' seemed to appear, in spite of being severely limited by having such 'little strength'. Finally, we arrive at 'Cool Court Chapel', Laodicea. This was the 'coolest' place around—'lukewarm', in fact, like the dreadful tepid water that flowed into the city. Here was no revitalising hot drink on a cold night, or a refreshing cold drink on a hot day. This was a church that had become as unpalatable as water from a stagnant pond, so far as Jesus was concerned.

Dr Jesus had different prescriptions for each of these patients, whom he loved so dearly and knew so well. His 'eyes like blazing fire' (Revelation 1:14) never miss a thing. Accordingly, we should be cautious when offered universal church panaceas, along the lines of 'What the church really needs is this available online for a mere £50 per month subscription'!

Reflection

Do you recognise your fellowship in any of these ancient churches? Do you see something of yourself? What can you do about it? Sadly, somehow or other, Jesus Christ ended up right outside one of these churches, as he can find himself outside our very lives, homes and families. Yet he still invites us to himself: 'Here I am! I stand at the door and knock. If anyone hears my voice and opens the door, I will come in and eat with him, and he with me' (3:20). Let's not keep the Lord of the universe waiting a moment longer for our response.

31 December

Supreme HQ

After this I looked, and there before me was a door standing open in heaven. And the voice I had first heard speaking to me like a trumpet said, 'Come up here, and I will show you what must take place after this.' At once I was in the Spirit, and there before me was a throne in heaven with someone sitting on it. And the one who sat there had the appearance of jasper and carnelian. A rainbow, resembling an emerald, encircled the throne...

Each of the four living creatures had six wings and was covered with eyes all around, even under his wings. Day and night they never stop saying: 'Holy, holy, holy is the Lord God Almighty, who was, and is, and is to come.' Whenever the living creatures give glory, honour and thanks to him who sits on the throne and who lives for ever and ever, the twenty-four elders fall down before him who sits on the throne, and worship him who lives for ever and ever. They lay their crowns before the throne and say:

You are worthy, our Lord and God,
to receive glory and honour and power,
for you created all things,
and by your will they were created
and have their being.'

Revelation 4:1–3, 8–11

I wept and wept because no-one was found who was worthy to open the scroll or look inside. Then one of the elders said to me, 'Do not weep! See, the Lion of the tribe of Judah, the Root of David, has triumphed. He is able to open the scroll and its seven seals.' Then I saw a Lamb, looking as if it had been slain, standing in the centre of the throne, encircled by the four living creatures and the elders. He had seven horns and seven eyes, which are the seven spirits of God sent out into all the earth…

And they sang a new song:

'You are worthy to take the scroll
and to open its seals,
because you were slain,
and with your blood you purchased men for God
from every tribe and language and people and nation.
You have made them to be a kingdom
and priests to serve our God,
and they will reign on the earth.'
Revelation 5:4–6, 9–10

The visions contained in Revelation 4 and 5 are not immediately accessible to most modern readers. However, as when we are viewing great works of art, sometimes we need to take a step or two back from the painting's details to see the larger canvas. So, what is the 'big picture' here? A number of things suggest themselves:

- The authority of the throne
- The glory of God
- The mystery of existence

- The centrality of worship
- The necessity of a redeemer

The theme of the throne occurs repeatedly in this book. It can refer to dark forces exercising their wanton power,[3] or others, like the elders in this vision, exercising authority to the glory of God. Primarily, however, 'throne' is used to assert the reign of the God who bears the title 'Almighty', which means 'ruler of all'. In other words, ultimate power resides with God, not with the persecutor, the evil forces ranged against the Church, or the whim or will of humanity. But is it not true that 'power tends to corrupt, and absolute power corrupts absolutely', according to Lord Acton's famous dictum?[4] For humans, that may be so, but not for God. His is a rule of holy love. This is part of his 'glory'. Although his holiness, echoing the song of the seraphim in Isaiah 6:3, is triply and solemnly asserted, his throne is encircled by a rainbow. This signifies his grace and love, and harks back to the story of Noah and God's commitment to keeping his promises of mercy (Genesis 9:12–17).

Increasingly in our day, science elucidates how things work, but the 'why' of existence is ultimately both a theological and philosophical quest. Why is there something rather than nothing? The answer here is clear: 'for you created all things, and by your will they were created and have their being' (4:11). In other words, the created sphere has a reason. It exists by the will of God. For instance, I understand that the indigenous North American rattlesnake's rattle shakes at 90 oscillations per second. If human beings had a similar metabolism, we would be able to run a full-length marathon in mere minutes. We know how the snake does that. The ultimate 'why', however, is beyond the competency even of a David Attenborough.

One of the major themes of both the Bible generally and the book of Revelation in particular is that of worship. During this period, the Emperor Domitian accrued to himself titles like 'Lord' and 'God'. It is much easier to keep an empire together if everyone either thinks you are divine or at least plays along with the charade by offering incense to your image in a suitable Roman town once a year. As the apostle Paul summarised it, there were those who had 'exchanged the truth of God for a lie, and worshipped and served created things rather than the Creator' (Romans 1:25). But for the early Christians, the very thought of offering worship to any other Master was unthinkable, since 'Jesus is Lord' was their basic confession and conviction. So Revelation is punctuated by doxology after doxology, as in these chapters, where God in Christ is worshipped, not the creature. Whom and why we worship is, therefore, far more important than how and where and when. When the former are in place, the latter should follow.

But how are we able to approach this holy, eternal, righteous and Almighty God? Who dare come before such a being? An older hymn expresses it like this:

Eternal Light! Eternal Light!
How pure the soul must be,
When, placed within thy searching sight,
It shrinks not, but with calm delight
Can live, and look on thee.[5]

Whose soul is that pure in the sight of God? The vision of the awesome Creator God of Revelation 4 is counterpoised with that of the Redeemer God in chapter 5. When it looks as if no one is worthy or able to reveal and fulfil the purposes of God, we are introduced to the lion king whose lamb-like sacrifice has bought and brought salvation to multitudes. This one has 'ransomed people for God... and they shall reign on the earth' (5:9–10, ESV). If that is true, then ultimately we cannot be doom-mongers about the future of the world, however changed it will eventually be.[6] To misquote a well-known phone advert, 'The future's bright, the future's Christ'—and, because of him, our future is bright, too. All our best days are ahead!

Reflection

Tonight is New Year's Eve, a good time to review an old year. How would you describe yours? Perhaps it would be appropriate to make a note of your 'triumphs and disasters'. For what are you especially grateful? Why not turn those items into songs of thanksgiving to God? What has been and maybe still is exceedingly painful? Make them your prayers. Before joining a rendition of 'Auld lang syne' later this evening, joining your heart and voice with the angels' song here in Revelation will get you off to one of the best starts of this or any year:

Then I looked and heard the voice of many angels, numbering thousands upon thousands, and ten thousand times ten thousand. They encircled the throne and the living creatures and the elders. In a loud voice they sang:

'Worthy is the Lamb, who was slain,
to receive power and wealth and wisdom and strength
and honour and glory and praise!'

Then I heard every creature in heaven and on earth and under the
earth and on the sea, and all that is in them, singing:
'To him who sits on the throne and to the Lamb
be praise and honour and glory and power,
for ever and ever!'
REVELATION 5:11–13

1 January

'Happy New Year, Dionysius!'

> But when the time had fully come, God sent his Son, born of a woman, born under law, to redeem those under law, that we might receive the full rights of sons. Because you are sons, God sent the Spirit of his Son into our hearts, the Spirit who calls out, 'Abba, Father.' So you are no longer a slave, but a son; and since you are a son, God has made you also an heir.
>
> Galatians 4:4–7

If you think his first name is unusual, just try his 'surname': Exiguus. It's the Latin for 'small, short, poor'. We could translate it as 'Dionysius the trifle'. Apparently, he gave himself the surname as a mark of humility (I trust he wasn't proud of it!). He was an obscure Scythian monk who lived in Rome in the sixth century. Yet every day he's remembered in the news, from *The Times* to the tabloids—every day, without exception. How come?

Very little is known about this monk's life, but he has left an indelible impression on Western history. He was tasked, we discover, with constructing a new calendar, which, in the

Roman world, had hitherto been based on the one instituted by Julius Caesar in 46BC, known as the Julian Calendar. Dionysius did his calculations and based his calendar on the year of the birth of Jesus. It is true that Pope Gregory XIII's calendar of 1582 made some adjustments to his calculations, but Dionysius' major impact on the world had been established.

Today, Dionysius, through the Gregorian calendar, holds sway. Alternative dates are, of course, used in other cultures, as you'll discover if you read, for instance, the *Jerusalem Post* (in 2012 the Jewish year is 5773). However, remarkably, every day of every year is a silent witness not to 'Dionysius the trifle' but to his Lord, Jesus the Son of God. That's quite a thought. An obscure Jewish peasant girl gives birth to a son, in a stable of all places, in a remote corner of the Roman Empire—and, over 2000 years after that birth, virtually every newspaper, news bulletin, cash dispenser, computer, mobile phone, stock exchange, bank and government bears witness to his coming through its use of the BC/AD calendar.

Of course, that child did not simply turn up out of nowhere and rather unexpectedly. One of the essay questions beloved of church historians, when I was an undergraduate many moons ago, ran something like this: 'Christianity was born into a world that favoured its growth. Discuss.' Dutifully, the diligent student would draw attention to the Greek culture that had provided a common language to the Roman world, which in turn had brought the Pax Romana, with its excellent roads and legal and communication systems. Finally, the Jewish faith had spread throughout the empire, complete with its scriptures available in the Greek tongue. All of those factors and more are contained in the phrase 'when the time had fully come'. The coming of this child had been long prepared.

That child, like Dionysius, also had a name—quite a number of names, in fact. In our reading today he is the 'Son', in the unique sense of being from the God-side of reality.[7] But we know him as Jesus (God the Rescuer), Christ (the longed-for Messiah and deliverer), Emmanuel (God with us) and the Lord, who has conquered death and deals with our sin, pride and prejudice, not in a display of awesome power but in self-giving love, on a cross, between two thieves.

AD1999; AD2012; AD2017... Now there lurks some more Latin: Anno Domini, 'the year of the Lord'. Indeed, the 'AD' is far more important than the numbers after it, whether they are 1912 or 2112 (that's not a typo: I have an eye on the future!). For 'AD' is a reminder that the coming of Jesus to Bethlehem is the fulcrum of history and the focus of eternity. Through his coming, we 'receive the full rights of sons', so we are part of God's family. We receive God's gift of his Holy Spirit, so we may know intimacy with God, 'the Spirit who calls out, "Abba, Father"'. Our slavery has been superseded and our future is brilliantly bright: 'God has made you also an heir'. This new year, whatever it holds, is still 'the Lord's year'. He who died for us is alive for evermore. He is our great contemporary, our living, loving, available Lord.

So is it exactly 2012 years ago, for instance, since Jesus was born in Bethlehem? Well, Dionysius may have been slightly out in his calculations. It makes little difference to the central truth: since Dionysius Exiguus, every year is a reminder of the first Christmas when the Son of Mary came to reveal the heart of God and redeem the world. Compared to that truth, Dionysius's slight miscalculation, like his name, is a mere 'trifle'.

Happy New Year, Dionysius! Happy New Year, whatever your name! Christ the Lord has come. And may Christ the Lord go with you through this year and always!

Reflection

Before Jesus came, the world was 'BC': 'before Christ'. Life without him can also be described as 'BC': Baffling and Confusing; Barren and Comfortless; Bland and Cold.

When we turn and return to him, life becomes 'AD': I'm Acquitted and Delivered; I'm Adopted and Desired; I'm Accepted and find a Destiny.

2 January

Does the future have a Church?

After this I looked and there before me was a great multitude that no-one could count, from every nation, tribe, people and language, standing before the throne and in front of the Lamb. They were wearing white robes and were holding palm branches in their hands. And they cried out in a loud voice: 'Salvation belongs to our God, who sits on the throne, and to the Lamb.' All the angels were standing round the throne and around the elders and the four living creatures. They fell down on their faces before the throne and worshipped God, saying: 'Amen! Praise and glory and wisdom and thanks and honour and power and strength be to our God for ever and ever. Amen!' Then one of the elders asked me, 'These in white robes—who are they, and where did they come from?' I answered, 'Sir, you know.' And he said, 'These are they who have come out of the great tribulation; they have washed their robes and made them white in the blood of the Lamb. Therefore, they are before the throne of God and serve him day and night in his temple; and he who sits on the throne will spread his tent over them. Never again will they hunger; never again will they thirst. The sun will not

beat upon them, nor any scorching heat. For the Lamb at the centre of the throne will be their shepherd; he will lead them to springs of living water. And God will wipe away every tear from their eyes.'
Revelation 7:9–17

The fastest-growing religion in the ancient world of the first century was the Imperial Cult, emperor worship. You could 'thank whatever gods may be'[8] so long as you annually offered incense and proclaimed 'Caesar as Lord'. As we noted a couple of days ago, this was impossible for Christians who asserted the Lordship of Jesus over everything.[9] Conflict, therefore, was inevitable. It still is in many parts of the world, where believers, in good conscience, remain true to Jesus and pay the price, sometimes with their very lives.

Today's focus on the future and the Church may not be the first question that is on our minds as a new year gets underway. Do I have a future? What about my job, health, mortgage or family, to say nothing about international security, the economy, global warming and a dozen other equally pressing and depressing matters?

At one level, it's really a question of focus on the hopes and dreams that shape us and give life meaning and purpose. For some, like Jean-Paul Sartre, such visions are ultimately illusory: 'Here we are, all of us, eating and drinking to preserve our precious existence, and… there is nothing, nothing, absolutely no reason for existing.'[10] More humorously, Yogi Berra, an American baseball star of yesteryear, said, 'We're lost, but we're making good time.'[11] If Revelation 4 and 5 reminded us that 'in the shadow of impending persecution…

an omnipotent and omniscient God is still in control',[12] chapter 7 assures us that, ultimately, God's people are safe and his purposes on track, come what may.

It's important to note the utter realism of this chapter. This great multitude had 'come out of the great tribulation', but found cleansing in God's sight through 'the blood of the Lamb', a metaphor for the sacrificial death of Jesus on the cross. Whatever else 'the great tribulation' may finally refer to, already, for millions of people alive today, life can only be described as 'great tribulation': war, famine, disease, disasters and finally death, and, so often, a world where tyrants rule and basic human rights are denied. For example, on 12 December 1938, Soviet leader Joseph Stalin signed 30 lists of death sentences. That same evening he proceeded to his private theatre, where he laughed and smiled his way through two comedies, having authorised the killing of 5000 victims, many of whom he knew personally. In addition, there have been countless other atrocities committed throughout the latter part of the 20th century alone: 'killing fields', 'ethnic cleansings' and genocide on a vast scale.

In stark contrast to all the horrors of a turbulent world, there is an amazingly positive vision presented here of what life will be like. 'Salvation belongs to our God' is short-hand for the saving activity and grace of God, which has accomplished his plan to have 'a great multitude... standing before the throne and in front of the Lamb'. God's promise to Abraham, centuries before, that he would be 'the father of many nations' (Genesis 17:4) now becomes 'mission accomplished'. Here these people find intimacy with God before his throne, provision for all their needs, protection from danger, and endless satisfaction that replaces all life's sadness as tears are wiped away.

Is the individual overlooked or lost in the crowd? Recently, I had lunch with a delightful woman in her 90s, named Sally, while I was at the annual Keswick Convention in Cumbria. She had first attended the convention as a babe in arms in 1918. During the course of our lunch, she produced magnificently clear black and white photographs from conventions held in her youth. Each picture showed large crowds outside the Convention Tent in Skiddaw Street—hundreds and hundreds of faces, and all so clear. But the most poignant for me was a scene from 1924. 'There's my father,' Sally proudly said. 'He was a steward. And next to him, that's me when I was six years old!' When we belong to Jesus, we too are part of a great multitude but, like Sally, we are never a nameless face in the crowd or just lost in the throng. Rather, each one of us is known, loved and welcomed by God. The prospect of my presence among that great multitude should fill me with breathless wonder and gratitude to God, and a renewed sense of dignity and destiny about all my tomorrows.

Does the future have a Church—that is, the people of God? You bet!

Reflection

Saviour, if of Zion's city
I through grace a member am,
Let the world deride or pity,
I will glory in thy Name:

Fading is the worldling's pleasure,
All his boasted pomp and show;
Solid joys and lasting treasure
None but Zion's children know.
JOHN NEWTON (1779)

3 January

Star Wars

A great and wondrous sign appeared in heaven: a woman clothed with the sun, with the moon under her feet and a crown of twelve stars on her head. She was pregnant and cried out in pain as she was about to give birth. Then another sign appeared in heaven: an enormous red dragon with seven heads and ten horns and seven crowns on his heads. His tail swept a third of the stars out of the sky and flung them to the earth. The dragon stood in front of the woman who was about to give birth, so that he might devour her child the moment it was born. She gave birth to a son, a male child, who will rule all the nations with an iron sceptre. And her child was snatched up to God and to his throne. The woman fled into the desert to a place prepared for her by God, where she might be taken care of for 1260 days.

And there was war in heaven. Michael and his angels fought against the dragon, and the dragon and his angels fought back. But he was not strong enough, and they lost their place in heaven. The great dragon was hurled down— that ancient serpent called the devil, or Satan, who leads the whole world astray. He was hurled to the earth, and his angels with him. Then I heard a loud voice in heaven say: 'Now have come the salvation and the power and the kingdom of our God, and the authority of his Christ. For the accuser of our brothers, who accuses them before our God day and night, has been hurled down. They overcame him by the blood of the Lamb and by the word of their testimony; they did not love their lives so much as to shrink from death. Therefore rejoice, you heavens and you who dwell in them! But woe to the earth and the sea, because the devil has gone down to you! He is filled with fury, because he knows that his time is short.'

When the dragon saw that he had been hurled to the earth, he pursued the woman who had given birth to the male child. The woman was given the two wings of a great eagle, so that she might fly to the place prepared for her in the desert, where she would be taken care of for a time, times and half a time, out of the serpent's reach. Then from his mouth the serpent spewed water like a river, to overtake the woman and sweep her away with the torrent. But the earth helped the woman by opening its mouth and swallowing the river that the dragon had spewed out of his mouth. Then the dragon was enraged at the woman and went off to make war against the rest of her offspring—those who obey God's commandments and hold to the testimony of Jesus.
Revelation 12

Who Framed Roger Rabbit? was a fantasy comedy film produced by Steven Spielberg in 1988. In it, cartoon characters directly interact with human beings. By the end of the film, you could leave the cinema believing Roger Rabbit to be as real as Bob Hoskins, one of the actors. In some ways, this chapter is a similarly brilliant interplay between real people and 'cartoon characters' that represent spiritual realities and dark forces. Some years ago, an insurance company used a clever advertising slogan to describe its attitude when claims arose: 'We won't make a drama out of a crisis'. But here the crisis facing these early Christians is presented as a drama. It is the original Star Wars, replete with sequels in which an Empire strikes back while the Church waits for the Return of Jesus.

In Film One, the first paragraph of our reading, we are introduced to some of the cast. Firstly, there is a woman, the Virgin Mary perhaps or, more likely, a symbol of the Church (see Isaiah 54:1). She has borne a son, in fulfilment of that ancient prophecy of Genesis 3:15.[13] Clearly, this is Jesus, but the in-between details of his life, death and resurrection are omitted as he is 'caught up to God' (v. 5, ESV), indicating his ascension. Next, we are introduced to 'an enormous red dragon' whose identity is clearly spelt out in the next section. He sweeps down 'a third of the stars', which in this type of literature usually means angels. This is the original Star Wars.

The second paragraph, Film Two, may be read in two ways. Do the events recorded look back to something that happened pre-temporally—that is, before our human time began?[14] Or does the ascension of Christ trigger some kind of spiritual chain reaction in the invisible heavenly places? Either option echoes a recurring biblical theme, stretching back to Genesis. 'The serpent', along with something monstrous, has entered the human race both generally and specifically, following 'the Fall'.[15] The subject of the demonic is not for the faint-hearted, but the message of this scene is greatly encouraging. Satan 'was not strong enough', so believers may overcome him through 'the blood of the Lamb'—that is, through the victory that Jesus secured on the cross. This element of the achievement of the cross is called *Christus Victor*. Through his death, resurrection and ascension to the throne, Jesus Christ has defeated the dark, evil powers ranged against the human race: he has 'disarmed the powers and authorities... triumphing over them by the cross' (Colossians 2:15).

So the foe is defeated and all is well? Not yet fully or finally. The Empire Strikes Back because Satan 'is filled with fury'. Now continuing war is conducted against the 'offspring' of the woman—her 'seed', the recurring theme that we have noted several times before. How can we recognise her offspring? They are the ones who march to a different drumbeat, obeying God and following Jesus. So is it finally down to their own tenacity, ingenuity and determination to get through this war?

The battle is intense because the devil knows that 'his time is short' and the Return of Jesus is expected, so he continues 'to make war' against believers. Meanwhile, and in spite of enemy pursuit, supernatural help is given to the woman. A 'great eagle', a metaphor for God's help (see Exodus 19:4), and the earth itself come to her rescue. Christian presence is maintained in God's world not because we deserve it or always get it right, or because our PR machine works well. Finally, it is because in Christ 'God is for us', by the power of his Holy Spirit (Romans 8:31). Such assurance is part of that wider 'testimony of Jesus' found in the Bible. Roger Rabbit and Star Wars are, of course, fictional; 'God for us' is 'the gospel truth'!

Reflection

'There are two equal and opposite errors into which our race can fall about the devils. One is to disbelieve in their existence. The other is to believe, and to feel an excessive and unhealthy interest in them. They themselves are equally pleased by both errors and hail a materialist or a magician with the same delight.'
C.S. LEWIS[16]

Which of those two errors do you feel more drawn towards? How do we keep a wise balance between 'blaming it all on the devil' and thinking it is 'all my fault'?

4 January

God rules, OK?

After this I heard what sounded like the roar of a great multitude in heaven shouting: 'Hallelujah! Salvation and glory and power belong to our God, for true and just are his judgments. He has condemned the great prostitute who corrupted the earth by her adulteries. He has avenged on her the blood of his servants.' And again they shouted: 'Hallelujah! The smoke from her goes up for ever and ever.' The twenty-four elders and the four living creatures fell down and worshipped God, who was seated on the throne. And they cried: 'Amen, Hallelujah!' Then a voice came from the throne, saying: 'Praise our God, all you his servants, you who fear him, both small and great!' Then I heard what sounded like a great multitude, like the roar of rushing waters and like loud peals of thunder, shouting: 'Hallelujah! For our Lord God Almighty reigns. Let us rejoice and be glad and give him glory! For the wedding of the Lamb has come, and his bride has made herself ready. Fine linen, bright and clean, was given her to wear.' (Fine linen stands for the righteous acts of the saints.) Then the angel said to me, 'Write: "Blessed are those who are invited to the wedding supper of the Lamb!"' And he added, 'These are the true words of God.'

Revelation 19:1–9

'The sovereignty of God' is a shorthand way to describe something of what is contained in the awesome statement, 'Hallelujah! For our Lord God Almighty reigns.' 'Almighty' means 'the ruler of everything', and it occurs ten times in the New Testament. Significantly, nine out of the ten references appear in Revelation, when it looks as if it might be 'game over' for the infant church of the first century. Both first- and 21st-century Christians need to be reminded regularly that God's plans and purposes are both on track and on time.

Let's be frank, however: it does not always look as if God is reigning, does it? John himself had been banished and imprisoned on the Island of Patmos, all sorts of challenges and problems assailed his churches,[17] and the future looked anything but promising against the might of imperial Rome. Perhaps some of this mirrors your personal experience. May-be there are factors 'imprisoning' you at present—family break-down, illness, difficulties in your local church, uncertainty in the workplace and so on. On a global scale recently, there have been earthquakes in Haiti, massive floods in Pakistan and a thousand tragedies which seem to deny that 'God rules'. If anyone asked him for a reason for his atheism before his conversion, C.S. Lewis's answer was as follows:

All stories will come to nothing: all life will turn out in the end to have been a transitory and senseless contortion upon the idiotic face of infinite matter. If you ask me to believe that this is the work of a benevolent and omnipotent spirit, I reply that all the evidence points in the opposite direction. Either there is no spirit behind the universe, or else a spirit indifferent to good and evil, or else an evil spirit.[18]

So is faith in an Almighty God merely wishful thinking or, worse still, sheer irrationality? The children's cartoon *Bob the Builder* regularly asks the question, 'Can he fix it?' and answers with a resounding, 'Yes, he can!' What about 'God the Builder'? The Christmas story tells of a God who has stepped on to a seemingly hopeless building site, a scene of devastation called planet earth, full of people with their own ideas, not his, on the way things should be. Can the Lord fix it? His cross, resurrection and final return are designed to do so, but it takes faith to believe that—the kind of faith without which 'it is impossible to please God' (Hebrews 11:6). The American preacher Ronald Dunn, himself no stranger to tragedy, following the suicide of his 18-year-old son, Ronnie, suggested that this is the type of faith that 'believes he is, even when it seems he isn't'.[19] Yes, of course, it requires faith to believe in God's sovereignty, but a moment or two's reflection on C.S. Lewis's alternatives to faith in the living God shows us that they also demand faith: I have to believe that there is no god, no purpose to life and so on.

There's an intriguing phrase used by grammarians to describe the word 'reigns' in our reading today: it is 'a timeless aorist'. Pardon? Expressed simply, it means, 'God did reign; God does reign; God will reign.' So here is a warning, a promise and an invitation. The warning that he 'will reign' reminds everyone of the Lord's commitment to establish his kingdom rule, and is therefore an urgent call to repentance—that is, a change of mind that leads to a change of direction, moving to God rather than from him. Evil will not triumph in the end, since God has determined that to Jesus 'every knee shall bow' (Revelation 20:7–15; Philippians 2:10–11).

The promise is that one day it will be evident that God 'did reign' through all the seeming chaos, misery and perplexity of life. If it helps us, I suspect that the Lord may replay the videos of our lives along the lines of *Match of the Day*, where we may see the highlights of our particular game of life: what goals we scored; what saves were made and what own goals we conceded, using technology and camera angles totally beyond our three-dimensional experience. The famous meditation that describes 'one set of footprints' on the beach at the times when we felt alone and abandoned (indicating, in fact, how the Lord carried us at those times) may be closer to reality than we ever dreamed.

So what is the invitation? It is to write over my life, 'God reigns', right here in my today, whatever my circumstances. If he does, then his sovereignty turns out to be not so much a theological conundrum as the source of my comfort in the trial, which enables me to keep going.

'Are we there yet?' is a question every parent has heard from a tired child on the car's back seat during a long journey. The reply 'Not yet' does not mean 'not ever'. Intriguingly, the only occurrence in the New Testament of the word 'Hallelujah' is found here, and then it is repeated three times. It almost feels like waiting for a bus: you wait for ages, and then four arrive together. Herein lies the challenge when life is really difficult. Can I still raise a 'Hallelujah' to express my trust in God, come what may?

Through all the changing scenes of life,
In trouble and in joy,
The praises of my God shall still
My heart and tongue employ.
NAHUM TATE AND NICHOLAS BRADY (1698)

'Are we there yet?' God's Almightiness is the best guarantee that we will arrive on time—his, not ours.

Reflection

This is the mystery of the divine government of history, whether on a national, domestic or individual level: the great and loving God is in control, and because he is truly sovereign he works out his purposes in his way, not ours (Isaiah 55:8). He offers no explanations but grants his people a sufficient insight into his ways, his character, his intentions and his changeless faithfulness so that, however dark the day, they can live by faith and be sustained by hope.

ALEC MOTYER[20]

NOTES

1   G.R. Beasley-Murray, *The Book of Revelation* (Marshall, Morgan & Scott, 1983), p. 27.

2   See www.messychurch.org.uk.

3   See Revelation 2:13; 13:2; 16:10.

4   Lord Acton in a letter to Bishop Mandell Creighton, 3 April 1887.

5   'Eternal Light! Eternal Light!' by Thomas Binney (1826).

6   See Revelation 21 and 22 and the reading for 6 January.

7   See the meditation for 24 December.

8   From 'Invictus' by William Ernest Henley (1875).

9   See the reading for 31 December.

10   Quoted by David Watson, *In Search of God* (Falcon, 1974), p. 32.

11 Yogi Berra, *The Yogi Book* (Workman, 1998), p. 51.

12 Robert H. Mounce, *The Book of Revelation* (Eerdmans, 1977), p. 130.

13 See the reading for 14 December.

14 Some find evidence of such a battle in Isaiah 14:12–15 and Ezekiel 28:11–19.

15 One of the reasons cited for the flood is connected to the 'sons of God', often interpreted as 'fallen angels,' and connected to passages like this one in Revelation. See Genesis 6:1–7. Obviously, certainty on such matters is not possible.

16 C.S. Lewis, *The Screwtape Letters* (Geoffrey Bles, 1942), p. 9.

17 See the reading for 30 December.

18 C.S. Lewis, *The Problem of Pain* (Collins, 1957), pp. 2–3.

19 Ronald Dunn wrote a helpful study on how God ministers to us through the challenges of life: *When Heaven is Silent* (Word, 1994).

20 Alec Motyer, *The Message of Exodus* (IVP, 2005), p. 19.

5 & 6 January

HOMEWARD BOUND

It is already the time of the end, and yet is not the end. This tension finds expression in the entire theology of Primitive Christianity. The present period of the Church is the time between the decisive battle, which has already occurred, and the 'Victory Day'.

OSCAR CULLMANN [1]

D-Day: Finished!

Later, knowing that all was now completed, and so that the
Scripture would be fulfilled, Jesus said, 'I am thirsty.' A jar of
wine vinegar was there, so they soaked a sponge in it, put
the sponge on a stalk of the hyssop plant, and lifted it to
Jesus' lips. When he had received the drink, Jesus said, 'It
is finished.' With that, he bowed his head and gave up his
spirit. Now it was the day of Preparation, and the next day
was to be a special Sabbath. Because the Jews did not want
the bodies left on the crosses during the Sabbath, they asked
Pilate to have the legs broken and the bodies taken down.
The soldiers therefore came and broke the legs of the first
man who had been crucified with Jesus, and then those of
the other. But when they came to Jesus and found that he
was already dead, they did not break his legs. Instead, one
of the soldiers pierced Jesus' side with a spear, bringing a
sudden flow of blood and water. The man who saw it has
given testimony, and his testimony is true. He knows that
he tells the truth, and he testifies so that you also may believe. These things happened so that the scripture would
be fulfilled: 'Not one of his bones will be broken,' and, as
another scripture says, 'They will look on the one they have
pierced.'

John 19:28–37

He had not yet become a Christian but he had been more than impressed by the sermon. In his native Cockney tongue, Chris related to me the one Greek word he had learned from the preacher, who had repeated it regularly throughout his address at that Good Friday service. 'Te-*tel*-estai,' he said. Or was it 'Te-tel-*esta*i'? Given either emphasis in pronunciation, the word was clear enough: *tetelestai*. It was the word on our Lord's dying lips, according to John's Gospel, translated 'It is finished'. Bishop J.C. Ryle commented that the word 'contains depths which no-one has ever completely fathomed… No one single meaning… exhausts the whole phrase. It is rich, full and replete with deep truths.'[2] Thankfully, however, some of the synonyms for 'finished' are illuminating: completed, fulfilled, accomplished, consummated, paid, realised, to name a few. So what does it mean for us as we are 'homeward bound'?

First, it is a reminder that scripture is being fulfilled. Three times within our reading, Old Testament scripture is quoted, and its fulfilment in the death of Christ is emphasised. Last century, the Nobel Peace Prize winner, theologian and medical doctor Albert Schweitzer (1875–1965) famously argued that Jesus expected the imminent inbreaking of the kingdom and the end of the world, as did the early Christians. However, in one way and another, he believed, the cross was not central to that kingdom's coming but was, rather, a 'Plan B'. But the Bible generally and the Gospels particularly insist that the crucifixion of Jesus was no accident or afterthought. John's Gospel speaks repeatedly of 'the hour' to which Jesus inexorably moved—the hour of his death. Through it he fulfilled what the sacrifices, sacred washings and special days of the Old Testament were always pointing towards—a community reconciled to God.[3]

Our second consideration is that the cross of Jesus has completed the work of salvation: it is a 'finished work'. The prophet Daniel foresaw a day that would finish transgression, put an end to sin, atone for wickedness and bring in everlasting righteousness (Daniel 9:24). That day arrived at Calvary. An Ulster friend of mine owns a decorating company. On one occasion, he was being conducted around Stormont, the home of the Northern Ireland Assembly, in preparation for submitting a quotation for its redecoration. When he entered the Great Hall, constructed entirely of Italian travertine marble, his guide pointed to the magnificent ceiling, commenting, 'George, you're not to touch that! It's a finished work.' So is the cross of Jesus. To attempt to add to it would be to detract from it. Jesus' death is more than sufficient to bring us forgiveness, peace with God and newness of life.

Finally, though certainly not exhaustively, 'finished' sounds a note of triumph, like an ancient army relaying via mountain-top messengers the good news to all at home: 'Victory has been secured!' However unpalatable it may seem to some sophisticated Christians in the developed world, the reality of dark evil forces terrorises many people in our world today. One of the reasons for the coming of Jesus was that 'by his death he might destroy him who holds the power of death—that is, the devil', along with all his 'work' (Hebrews 2:14; 1 John 3:8). Again, 'on that cross he discarded the cosmic powers and authorities like a garment; he made a public spectacle of them and led them as captives in his triumphal procession' (Colossians 2:15, NEB). Hell and all its forces, we might say, have received their deathblow. Jesus did not say, 'I am finished'. They are!

At 4:15am on 5 June 1944, ensconced in Southwick House, Hampshire, the centre for Operation Overlord, General Dwight D. Eisenhower uttered three famous words that would unleash the largest amphibious invasion of all time: 'OK... Let's go!' Within a day, men and machines in their thousands were swarming the beaches of Normandy. 'D-Day' had arrived. The liberation of Europe had begun. At one level, the war was over. In reality, there were still countless battles to fight, but the decisive turning point of World War II had arrived. From there on, it was simply a matter of time until Victory Day arrived. Are you battered, bruised and battle-weary now? Look up! Our full and final 'salvation is nearer now than when we first believed' (Romans 13:11).

Reflection

Christian existence is lived out between the 'D-Day' of Christ's cross and resurrection, and the 'V-Day' of his final return. In what ways does that help or challenge your Christian living today?

6 January

V-Day: Welcome home!

Then I saw a new heaven and a new earth, for the first heaven and the first earth had passed away, and there was no longer any sea. I saw the Holy City, the new Jerusalem, coming down out of heaven from God, prepared as a bride beautifully dressed for her husband. And I heard a loud voice from the throne saying, 'Now the dwelling of God is with men, and he will live with them. They will be his people, and God himself will be with them and be their God. He will wipe every tear from their eyes. There will be no more death or mourning or crying or pain, for the old order of things has passed away.' He who was seated on the throne said, 'I am making everything new!' Then he said, 'Write this down, for these words are trustworthy and true.' He said to me: 'It is done. I am the Alpha and the Omega, the Beginning and the End. To him who is thirsty I will give to drink without cost from the spring of the water of life.'
Revelation 21:1–6

The politician, author and broadcaster Lord Boothby (1900–1986) reputedly summarised his views on the afterlife as follows: 'The thought of a spiritual Boothby, seated on a cloud of cotton wool, playing a harp for ever and ever, has for me strictly limited appeal.' If such be humanity's ultimate destiny, then no wonder 'everybody wants to go to heaven but nobody wants to die!' Indeed, the prospect of such a bland eternal state makes us fear that we may be bored to death. What a marvellous corrective is the seer's vision in these concluding chapters of scripture. As someone has expressed it, if 'hope is the ability to hear the music of the future and faith the ability to dance to it today', then welcome indeed to the show!

The chapter opens with a rendition of a 'New World Symphony', celebrating the arrival of 'a new heaven and a new earth'. Now the biblical use of 'heaven' is somewhat flexible, covering a range of meanings, including God himself, the atmosphere, the invisible realm of spiritual reality, where we go when we die, and, as here, the final state of things.[4] The long promised 'new heaven and a new earth'[5] have finally arrived. Here, The Incredible Journey, begun in a garden aeons before, is finally completed. Humanity's lot of mourning, pain and death on a ravaged earth is superseded by a new world where 'every tear' is finally wiped away. How is that accomplished? By the God who makes 'everything new'. Tragically, not everyone has joined in the 'new song' of God's redeeming grace (Revelation 5:9)—preferring, to the end, their own discord and cacophony (21:8, 27).

But why a 'new earth'? Wouldn't going to heaven be enough? For the individual's immediate *post mortem* state, the answer would be 'Yes, of course!' (see 2 Corinthians 5: 8–9; Philippians 1:23). But 'No' is an equally appropriate response: the ultimate hope of Christian faith is the resurrection of the body that is based firmly on Christ's own resurrection (1 Corinthians 15). The eternal state is not to be a 'shadow of my former self': it is to be fully human again, an embodied life in which, quite literally, we may 'run and not grow weary… walk and not be faint' (Isaiah 40:31).

If humanity's history started in a garden back in Genesis 2, its destiny culminates in a city, albeit a garden-city, in Revelation. Here we find security, for the city is metaphorically protected by high walls and gates; community, for nations and kings are found within, with old divisions gone and all enjoying the light of God; and vitality, summarised by the removal of the curse and access again to 'the tree of life'.[6] Here is the ultimate restoration of all that was lost by our first parents,[7] and far more beside. Unlike them, we are not banished from Eden but welcomed to a paradise where, by God's grace, we 'reign for ever and ever' (Revelation 22:5).

Does the foregoing sound a little like 'pie in the sky when you die'? If so, we need to hear especially the angel's reassurance: 'These words are trustworthy and true' (22:6). Are we simply to 'take it on trust'—or in 'blind faith', as some would see it—and without anything to corroborate such a future?

There's a final, vital melody heard from this city, which is in stark contrast to so much of the disharmony that the Bible has recorded. It is actually the central reason for the symphony of grace that has been repeatedly played throughout the Bible for those who cared to tune in, especially when humanity's cacophony threatened to drown out every note of music but its own shrill sound. It is the harmony of a restored relationship with God himself. For, as we have seen during our long journey, the most tragic part of the humanity's lot is that we lost our vision of God. Even when we thought we desired it, since the Fall 'no one may see me and live,' says the Lord (Exodus 33:20). However, Jesus promised that the pure in heart would 'see God' (Matthew 5:8), and here, at last, God's servants again 'see his face' (Revelation 22:4). Finally and wonderfully, harmony has been restored between the Creator and his creation. This direct visual perception of the living God is often termed the 'beatific vision'. No longer do 'we see but a poor reflection as in a mirror'. Rather, it is now 'face to face' (1 Corinthians 13:12). Here is the climax of the great song and the conclusion of The Incredible Story. Indeed, it is the final homecoming: 'The dwelling-place of God is now among the people, and he will dwell with them. They will be his people, and God himself will be with them and be their God' (Revelation 21:3, TNIV).

In *The Last Battle*, C.S. Lewis captures something of the breathtaking wonder of what lies in store, in his description of the true Narnia into which, at the last, his adventurers enter:

All life in this world and their adventures in Narnia had only been the cover and the title page: as at last they were beginning Chapter One of the Great Story which no-one on earth has read; which goes on forever; in which every chapter is better than the one before.[8]

Reflection

For all the saints, who from their labours rest,
Who Thee by faith before the world confessed,
Thy name, O Jesus, be for ever blessed.
Hallelujah! Hallelujah!

But lo! There breaks a yet more glorious day;
The saints triumphant rise in bright array;
The King of glory passes on His way.
Hallelujah! Hallelujah!

From earth's wide bounds, from ocean's farthest coast,
Through gates of pearl streams in the countless host,
Singing to Father, Son, and Holy Ghost—
Hallelujah! Hallelujah!

WILLIAM WALSHAM HOW (1864)

Postscript

On 14 February 1990, as the Voyager 1 spacecraft was leaving the edges of our solar system, already some four billion miles from our world, NASA engineers turned it around for one last look at planet earth. The resulting image captured earth as a tiny point of light, 'a pale blue dot' only 0.12 pixels in size, in the centre of scattered rays of light. The picture inspired Carl Sagan, the famous astronomer and cosmologist, to comment as follows:

Look again at that dot. That's here. That's home. That's us. On it everyone you love, everyone you know, everyone you ever heard of, every human being who ever was, lived out their lives. The aggregate of our joy and suffering, thousands of confident religions, ideologies, and economic doctrines, every hunter and forager, every hero and coward, every creator and destroyer of civilisation, every king and peasant, every young couple in love, every mother and father, hopeful child, inventor and explorer, every teacher of morals, every corrupt politician, every 'superstar', every 'supreme leader', every saint and sinner in the history of our species lived there—on a mote of dust suspended in a sunbeam.

The earth is a very small stage in a vast cosmic arena. Think of the rivers of blood spilled by all those generals and emperors so that, in glory and triumph, they could become the momentary masters of a fraction of a dot. Think of the endless cruelties visited by the inhabitants of one corner of this pixel on the scarcely distinguishable inhabitants of some other corner, how frequent their misunderstandings, how eager they are to kill one another, how fervent their hatreds.

Our posturings, our imagined self-importance, the delusion that we have some privileged position in the universe, are challenged by this point of pale light. Our planet is a lonely speck in the great enveloping cosmic dark. In our obscurity, in all this vastness, there is no hint that help will come from elsewhere to save us from ourselves.[9]

Sagan both elegantly and seamlessly moves from scientific observation to the introduction, ever so subtly, of his own worldview: 'In all this vastness, there is no hint that help will come from elsewhere to save us from ourselves.' But it is precisely here that the Christian assertion that 'God was Man in Palestine'[10] protests most loudly. There is more than a hint that help has come to save us from ourselves. The Old Testament scholar and missiologist Christopher Wright has an altogether different way of addressing our human predicament, as he summarises the Bible's message:

As has been well documented, every human worldview is an outworking of some narrative. We live out of the story or stories we believe to be true, the story or stories that 'tell it like it is,' we think. So what does it mean to live out of this story? Here is The Story, the grand universal narrative that stretches from creation to new creation, and accounts for everything in between. This is The Story that tells us where we have come from, how we got to be here, who we are, why the world is in the mess it is, how it can be (and has been) changed, and where we are ultimately going. And the whole story is predicated on the reality of this God and the mission of this God. He is the originator of the story, the teller of the story, the prime actor in the story, the planner and guide of the story's plot, the meaning of the story and its ultimate completion. He is its beginning, end and centre. It is the story of the mission of God, of this God and no other.[11]

On 13 October 2010, as millions worldwide watched with rapt attention, Florencio Avalos was the first to emerge from a Chilean mine, hoisted to the surface in a specially constructed capsule named 'Phoenix', at a location called 'Camp Hope'. He and 32 fellow miners had been trapped, 2000 feet underground, for 69 days. The operation to rescue all 33 men had been amazingly complex but carefully planned and brilliantly executed. The scenes of joy were overwhelming as each miner was brought to the surface, reunited with loved ones and greeted by Chile's President Sebastian Pinera, who remarked that life had defeated death, and hope had triumphed over anguish. Help from 'up there' on the surface had reached 'down to the depths' to rescue and save.

Likewise, help from outside of ourselves is required to rescue us from our personal subterranean prisons, of whatever kind they may be. The God of Abraham and Isaac, kings and prophets, priests and apostles has, in Jesus Christ, made the Incredible Journey from eternity to time, from heaven to earth and from a throne to a cross, all carefully planned and brilliantly executed, right on time. From that rescue mission we learn that we are not accidents but products of a loving Creator's hand. We are not insignificant but we are people redeemed at infinite cost through Jesus, God's 'gift too wonderful for words' (2 Corinthians 9:15, LB). So we are not alone but inhabit a world to which Emmanuel, 'God with us', personally came—a world that, through his Spirit, he has never left. We matter, and so does everyone and everything else because of this wonderful, amazing, living God. When we believe the 'old, old story of Jesus and his love'[12] and enter 'the capsule of Christ', as those Chilean miners entered their 'Phoenix', we discover that we are on our personal Incredible Journey; we are homeward bound to a world where the light of God dispels all our darkness. One day, like those scenes of joy from 'Camp Hope', the journey will culminate in grand reunions and a welcome from the King of kings. What a story that is. What a story that will be!

NOTES

1 Oscar Cullmann, *Christ and Time* (SCM, 1962), p. 145.
2 J.C. Ryle, *Expository Thoughts on the Gospels*, Vol 4 (Baker, 1979), p. 322.
3 The letter to the Hebrews repeatedly emphasises this theme. See, for example, Hebrews 9:23—10:10.
4 See Luke 15:18 (compare NIV with REB); Psalm 8:3; Ephesians 6:12; Luke 23:43; 2 Corinthians 12:2, 4.
5 See Isaiah 65:17; 66:22; 2 Peter 3:13.
6 See Revelation 21:12–14, 23–26; 22:2–3.
7 See readings for 12 and 13 December.
8 Lewis, *The Last Battle*, p. 165.
9 See Carl Sagan, 'Pale blue dot', 1994, www.planetary.org/explore/topics/voyager/pale_blue_dot.html. I am grateful to my colleague at Moorlands College, Alistair McKitterick, for drawing my attention to this website.
10 From the brilliant poem 'Christmas' by Sir John Betjeman (1906–84).
11 Christopher J.H. Wright, *The Mission of God* (IVP, 2006), p. 533.
12 'Tell me the old, old story' by Katherine Hankey (1866).

Study Guide

This book has been written primarily for individuals to read daily through the season of Advent. However, it can also be helpfully used in a small group setting where members are following the readings and reflections each day. The questions below are based on each week's readings and are designed to prompt both further individual reflection and thoughtful discussion and prayer.

1–7 December: Starting out

1 'The Bible tells us who created the world, science tells us how.' How far would you agree with that statement?
2 On his 2010 visit to the UK, Pope Benedict XVI called on everyone, no matter what their faith, to uphold the dignity of each and every person. Is that call a legitimate outworking of being 'made in the image of God', would you say?
3 'Stewardship', for a Christian, has been defined as wise use of our talents, our time and our treasure. Which do you find most difficult to manage and why?
4 Marriage is more about being the right kind of person than finding 'the right person'. Would you agree? How can you help marriages in crisis in your church or social network?

Prayer

Father, grant me the grace to use whatever gifts and talents I have to promote your kingdom each day of my life. In Jesus' name, Amen.

8–14 December: Crashing badly

1 The Lord's Prayer reminds us to pray, 'Lead us not into temptation.' What practical steps have you found helpful in avoiding your particular weaknesses?

2 'Because people have lost "the fear of God" they behave like they do.' Is that the only reason why humans behave as badly as they do at times? In contrast, what explains 'good' behaviour in a fallen world, do you think?

3 Can you share any experiences of why and when you experienced a sense of alienation from God and/or people? How has the gospel of Christ helped you overcome that sense of estrangement?

4 Have you put in place all necessary arrangements for your eventual death—a will; clearly communicating your wishes for your funeral; making wise financial decisions while you can; being forgiven and forgiving others; telling those you love that you love them? Most of all, have you found peace with God through our Lord Jesus Christ?

Prayer

Lord, I live in a broken world, and I myself am weak and apt to stray. Fill me with the power of your Holy Spirit so that I may be part of your solution for this world's ills and not just more of its problem. In the name of Christ my Lord, Amen.

15–21 December: Detouring often

1 In addition to the seven Old Testament characters we have considered this week, who else would you add to the list of those who prepared the way for the coming of Jesus? Why do you think your 'addition' is important?

2 We suggested that Joseph's career could be summarised as 'from pit to prison to palace', and provides a model of Christ. Are there other parts of his life that do so? How far is Joseph a parallel to our lives as he heads for an ultimate 'happy ending'?

3 Many people assume that the Ten Commandments are like an exam paper: only three out of ten questions are to be addressed! Which ones do you find the most difficult and the most helpful? Why?

4 We noted that King David, like us all, was a mixture of 'triumphs and disasters' in his personal life. Some of us feel more encouraged by his disasters because God still stuck by him; others of us are more inspired by his triumphs to go and fight our 'Goliaths'. Which side of his character do you prefer and why?

Prayer

Father, thank you for choosing such unlikely and unpromising people to forward your kingdom on earth—Abraham, Moses, David and others—and even people like me. To you be the glory through Jesus Christ our Lord, Amen.

22–28 December: Arriving on time

1 What is your favourite part of the Christmas story? Can you attempt to tell it simply in your group so that a junior school assembly, for instance, would get the message?
2 Why is the incarnation the most spectacular miracle in the Bible? How can Jesus be both 'God and man' at the same time?
3 Joseph is often an 'unsung hero' in the Christmas story, yet he displayed great courage and amazing obedience. How far is he an ideal model for anyone in a stepfamily? Pause and pray especially for people you know who are in such families, for similar courage, patience, tact and love.
4 Astrology and other occultic practices are a growth industry in the UK today, Hallowe'en being a huge money-spinner, for instance. Is it all harmless 'fun'? Do the wise men as star-gazers give it legitimacy? If not, why not?

Prayer
Lord, thank you that your purpose of sending Jesus to this world was long-planned, carefully monitored, patiently implemented and brilliantly executed on time. Praise be to you, Almighty Father, for your amazing gift of Jesus, your own eternal Son, Amen.

29 December–4 January: Journeying on

1 Undoubtedly, the book of Revelation is not immediately easy to understand. However, its 'big message' assures us that God's ultimate purposes for this world are going to be fulfilled. Can you recall verses both in Revelation and

elsewhere that remind us of that truth? Should Christians therefore always be optimists, even in a world threatened by wars, famines and global warming?

2 Jesus Christ, from the very first chapter, dominates the book of Revelation. What titles (such as 'Son of Man' or 'Lamb') are ascribed to him, and what do they mean for us as his people?

3 Is being 'Messy Church' inevitable? Are there things in our local church that we need to 'clean up' and other things that are best just left alone? Can you illustrate and suggest ways forward? Why not enumerate your top five 'must haves' for your local church's effectiveness to be increased, and five areas that you would abandon immediately if that would aid the process?

4 Conflict is inevitable in the Christian life, as Revelation graphically illustrates. What resources are available to arm us for the battles of life? (You may wish, for instance, to meditate on Ephesians 6:10–18.)

Prayer

Lord Jesus Christ, you are the theme of the angels' song, the joy of heaven and your Father's delight. You who fill the whole cosmos by your Spirit, please fill me with your life and love in order to serve others, in your name, Amen.

5–6 January: Homeward bound

1 How helpful or otherwise is the analogy that the Christian life is lived between the 'D-Day' of the cross and the 'V-Day' of the Lord's return?

2 Since the Christian life is lived in both the 'now' and the 'not yet', can you list what we definitely have 'now' in Christ and what is 'not yet', for which we therefore wait? Should we expect more of the 'not yet' in our 'now'— things like healing, for example? Can you suggest others?
3 If a new heaven and a new earth are coming, should we therefore be indifferent to this present world? If not, why not?

Prayer

Gracious heavenly Father, thank you for the joy of Christmas; for the great truth that you were in Christ reconciling the world to yourself; that through Jesus you intend to make all things new; and that in the here and now your purposes are on track till the day your will is done on earth as it is in heaven. To Father, Son and Holy Spirit, one God, be glory both now and for ever more, Amen.

ENJOYED READING THIS ADVENT BOOK?

Did you know BRF publishes a new Lent and Advent book each year? All our Lent and Advent books are designed with a daily printed Bible reading, comment and reflection. Some can be used in groups and contain questions which can be used in a study or reading group.

Previous Advent books have included:

Pilgrims to the Manger, Naomi Starkey	Ref 978 1 84101 709 9, £7.99
Shock and Awe, Ian Coffey	Ref 978 1 84101 641 2, £6.99
A Handful of Light, Michael Mitton	Ref 978 1 84101 247 6, £7.99
Beginnings and Endings, Maggi Dawn	Ref 978 1 84101 566 8, £7.99

If you would like to be kept in touch with information about our forthcoming Lent or Advent books, please complete the coupon below.

❏ Please keep me in touch by post with forthcoming Lent or Advent books
❏ Please email me with details about forthcoming Lent or Advent books

Email address: _____

Name _____

Address_____

_____

_____

Postcode_____

Telephone_____

Signature _____

Please send this completed form to:

Freepost RRLH-JCYA-SZX
BRF, 15 The Chambers,
Vineyard, Abingdon,
OX14 3FE, United Kingdom

Tel. 01865 319700
Fax. 01865 319701
Email: enquiries@brf.org.uk

www.brf.org.uk

PROMO REF: END/ADVENT11

BRF is a Registered Charity

For more information, visit the **brf** website at **www.brf.org.uk**

THE WAY OF THE DESERT

Daily Bible readings through Lent to Easter

Andrew Watson

In the Bible the desert is a place of punishment and discipline, but also of blessing and love's reawakening. Both Jesus and the people of Israel before him spent time in the desert, learning what it meant to be chosen and loved and holy. Yet while the people of the exodus frequently got it wrong, providing some cautionary tales for us to learn from, Jesus himself constantly got it right, offering a perfect model for us to follow.

In *The Way of the Desert* Andrew Watson takes us on a Lenten journey from Ash Wednesday to Easter Day, from the parting of the Red Sea to Israel's entry into the promised land. Combining these Old Testament scriptures with insight from the Gospels, he reveals the continuing relevance of the exodus story to all who would seek to follow Christ.

ISBN 978 1 84101 798 3 £7.99   Available from November 2011 Available from your local Christian bookshop or, in case of difficulty, direct from BRF using the order form opposite. You may also order from the website www.brfonline.org.uk.